STEP SPIRIT

THE 12 STEPS AS A SPIRITUAL PROGRAM

Catherine Chapman, O.P.

PAULIST PRESS
New York/Mahwah, N.J.

Acknowledgment: The 12-Steps are found in "How it Works" in *Alcoholics Anonymous*, 1976, Alcoholics Anonymous World Services, Inc., pp. 59–60. The chapter headings of chapters 3–14 are the 12-Steps.

Library of Congress Cataloging-in-Publication Data

Chapman, Catherine, 1952–
   Step spirit: the 12 steps as a spiritual program/by Catherine Chapman.
      p. cm.
   ISBN 0-8091-3340-7 (pbk.)
    1. Twelve-step programs—Religious aspects—Christianity.
   2. Spiritual life—Christianity. I. Title.
   BV4501.2.C476   1992
   248.8′6—dc20
                                     92-19817
                                      CIP

Published by Paulist Press
997 Macarthur Boulevard
Mahwah, New Jersey 07430

Printed and bound in the
United States of America

CONTENTS

A WORD OF THANKS

This book began at St. John Vianney Catholic Church in Houston, Texas, with weekly meetings of the "Monday Night Miracles." Each member of that group, especially those who were able to complete those nine months, gave me the hope this program was gift and healing. With my thanks and prayers I dedicate this book to you, the original "Monday Night Miracles."

My thanks also to Tom Blocher, M.D. and Dee Murray, M.S.W. of the New Spirit substance abuse treatment program of Houston, Texas. At New Spirit, this program, which began with the "Monday Night Miracles," became "Step Spirit" and was used in both an inpatient and outpatient psychiatric setting.

Gratefully I acknowledge the work of Martha Wilson, Donna Kowalski and Mary Greenslade. They read the original manuscript and helped me tremendously with their praise and comments. Donna Pollard, O.P. was there as proofreader and supporter. My thanks to you and to the many of you who cheered me on.

1

INTRODUCTION

Twelve-Step programs appear to be pervasive. Almost every support group seems to be based upon the 12-Steps of Alcoholics Anonymous. No matter what the problem—substance abuse, sexual abuse, compulsive shopping, compulsive gambling, compulsive sex, emotional abuse—people are discovering the 12-Steps can give a structure for recovery.

The 12-Steps appear simple when first read, but they are deceptively simple. Working each Step involves great personal commitment, opening the individual to a deep inner change. Changing life patterns is not only very difficult, but also very risky, because something deep within us rebels against changing ourselves. Perhaps resistance to change stems from a false belief that we are near-perfect beings. Or, perhaps, the resistance is due to our fear of the unknown. After all, we do know what our life is like now. What if it becomes worse if we change?

Change involves risk and that can be very scary. Major risks are made easier with support. The 12-Steps is a powerful program providing group support and, by helping us tap into our spiritual resources, discover God, our Higher Power.

Step Spirit is a process of studying the 12-Steps by examining the spiritual dynamics of each Step. Although this process is similar to other kinds of Step study, greater emphasis is given to spirituality and to the interweaving of the emotional and spiritual development of the individual.

Anyone who works a 12-Step program works a spiritual program, even if initially unaware of this. The 12-Steps follow the progression of spiritual development as found in traditional Judeo-Christian spirituality. We begin to grow spiritually when we become aware of our own finiteness and our powerlessness over people, places and things (Step 1). We realize we have certain limitations. As much as we try, we cannot do all we want to do by ourselves. Our sense of powerlessness over people, places and things leads us to look for One who has power, who is more powerful than ourselves (Step 2). Most people in the Western world call this Higher Power God.

Once we come to believe in God, we are then faced with the question of trusting this God. To continue our spiritual growth we decide to turn our wills and our lives over to God (Step 3). We become connected to a God who not only is love, but also loves us. When we find love we begin to examine the times in our lives when we have failed to love (Step 4). This Step brings us great pain. We feel, in varying degrees, guilt and shame. To help break the shame and heal our pain we admit what we have done and tell God and someone we trust about our failings (Step 5). Of course, we do not want to hurt people, or ourselves, anymore; therefore, we want to change those characteristics within us that brought us to cause such pain (Step 6). We ask the One more powerful than ourselves, God, to help us change (Step 7). However, our spiritual growth does not allow us to stop there. We want to rectify in some way the harm we have done (Steps 8, 9). As we experience a serenity we may have never before experienced, we do all we can to continue the path of growth and development (Step 10), including improving our relationship with God (Step 11). Since this program has worked so well for us we want to let others know what has happened to us (Step 12).

Although this is a spiritual program, it is not a religious program. You do not need to have been raised in any particular religion. You do not even need to have a positive outlook toward religion, although it is helpful. Religion and spirituality, although they can be complementary, are different. Religion involves a certain set of beliefs, customs, rituals, rules and laws relating in various ways to the worshipping of God. Spirituality is that part within ourselves that yearns to go beyond ourselves and touch the Other. Religion may provide a vehicle for our connecting with God.

People who have had negative experiences with traditional religion are often reluctant to begin this program. Again, the 12-Steps is not a religious program. There are not any designated or ordained authorities in a 12-Step group. No one person has a higher rank than another. The "authorities" in your 12-Step meetings are people who, like yourselves, were or are in deep emotional pain. The only way they differ from those of you beginning the 12-Steps is they are farther along in their journey. They have compassion for you in your pain. Many times the other group members see themselves in your pain, and are willing to share the wisdom they have gained as they have worked through their pain. As you come to know people who have been working the 12-Steps you will notice the serenity they have. You will come to know that through the Steps we open ourselves to healthy relationships with ourselves, others, our world and God, our Higher Power. We do this by developing our own spirituality.

As you read the 12-Steps you will notice each Step is written in the plural. The 12-Steps is a community-based program. Although each individual is the only one who can work her or his personal program, we gain support and benefits from the community of those who have worked and are now working the 12-Steps. We need to hear the stories and wisdom of those who encountered roadblocks to their growth, and how they made progress. We need to know there is hope and that we are not alone. Group members can help provide that hope when we reach a barrier to our growth. If we work the 12-Steps alone, we may isolate ourselves when we reach such a barrier and consider ourselves failures. Find a 12-Step group suitable for your needs and become an active member (AA, Al-anon, Adult Children of Alcoholics, Co-dependents Anonymous, Emotions Anonymous, and many, many more).

The purpose of Step Spirit is to give individuals information on the spiritual dynamics of the 12-Steps and suggestions for various prayer experiences to aid in the quest for growth and healing. It is imperative to realize that to receive benefit from the Steps, one must work these Steps daily. In a way, these Steps are "spiritual exercises." Like any type of exercise, to derive maximum benefit, these must be practiced or, as is said, "worked" as regularly as we care for our most basic needs.

The individual Steps are not placed in a random order, but are worked one at a time with each Step being the foundation for the next Step. (The only Step that can be worked "out of order" is the Eleventh Step. Step 11, which is implied in Steps 2 and 3, helps us open ourselves to the healing love and power of our Higher Power, God.) By working these Steps one by one we lay a strong foundation for our program that will keep us moving toward our goal of serenity and peace.

Take your time going through the Steps. There is no reason to rush. This is a self-paced program. There is no reward for finishing this program faster than anyone else. The truth is, you never do finish. Work the Steps as completely as you can at this time, and continue to work them day by day for the rest of your life.

There is no "wrong" way to work these Steps. Just work them as honestly as you can. By beginning to learn about the Steps, and by trying to follow the principles contained in them, you will be working them correctly. Listen to others in your

12-Step group describe how they worked the Steps. Some of what they have learned will be helpful to you. That which is not helpful can be left at the meeting. "Take what you need and leave the rest." When you become frustrated in your progress remember that wherever you are is exactly where you should be. As is often said, "Do not compare your inside with someone else's outside." You are your own measure of yourself.

ESPECIALLY FOR WOMEN

You will find at the end of each chapter, just before the Prayer Experiences, a section entitled "Especially for Women." This section contains an elaboration of that particular Step as it pertains to the questions of women I have accompanied on part of their journey. Although men may also find this information helpful, I do hope this section eases the frustration some women have with the 12-Steps.

Tools for Recovery

As you work the Steps using Step Spirit, you will find several basic exercises are used. Below are descriptions of the various tools or techniques you may wish to use as you travel your path to recovery.

JOURNALING

Most of us, when we go forth on a journey, would like to have a record of our trip. Later we can look at the photographs, recall the events and experience again the forgotten emotions.

Beginning a 12-Step program is also beginning a journey. Many people find it very helpful to keep a record of their journey. One way is through journaling. In journaling we record our thoughts, feelings and images and the meaning they contain for us. Often journaling enables us to sort through thoughts and feelings, or even to discover feelings that are deeply buried.

There is pain, productive pain, but pain nonetheless, when we work the Steps. We get in touch with those destructive attitudes, values and beliefs we hold but don't want to admit to ourselves. Through them we have hurt others. Frequently, painful feelings and events long buried come to our consciousness. Journaling helps us sort through the pain and the myriad of emotions beneath the pain. Journaling also allows us to know where we have been and, perhaps, gives us an idea of where we might be going.

MEDITATION AND PRAYER EXPERIENCES

Meditation is an important part of the Step Spirit process. When we meditate we quiet our minds and hearts. We attempt to put aside the cares, activities and even thoughts that can distract us from what is happening deep within us. So often the tumult surrounding us can keep us from listening to the Self deep within begging to be known to our conscious selves. The Self within is our true Self, unlike the artificial self we display to the world as a disguise.

When we meditate in the manner described below, we come in contact with the Self. Once we establish contact we can begin our recovery, our recovery of Self. The meditation experiences given facilitate the healing of the wounded Self by awakening ourselves to God. We then allow God to love us and heal us.

There are several guidelines many people find helpful when beginning meditation experiences. These suggestions may be of help to you; if not, try something else. If you need other ideas you might want to broach the subject in one of your 12-Step meetings and discover what is helpful to others. The members of your support group may not have the answer for you, but the group does contain a wealth of information that may lead you to discover your own answer.

Meditation, especially the experiences described after each Step, takes both quiet and time. Daily set aside a block of time, beginning with 10–15 minutes. Find some quiet place you can designate as your prayer or meditation area. Unplug the telephone, turn off the radio and TV. Assemble in your meditation area all you need—comfortable chair, journal, pen, meditation book, candle, etc. When all is as ready as it will be (there are few perfect situations) it is time to begin.

After each Step you will find one or more suggested exercises to use for prayer and meditation. Most of these experiences ask you to visualize or image certain situations. For the visualization experiences, I usually use a particular exercise as a beginning and work other experiences from this basic situation. If you have not previously done any type of visualization you will need to take some time to feel comfortable with these experiences. I initially needed someone to lead me through the exercises. You may find it helpful to have someone read the experience to you. Another alternative is to tape the experience yourself and play it back during your time of prayer and meditation. After each sentence allow yourself time to image what is being said. There is no need to rush through the exercise. As you gain experience you will relax much more quickly. Of course, if a particular image doesn't suit you, create one that does. What is written here is simply a model for you to form your own experiences.

Many people, like myself, find it difficult to form definite images. In this instance just try to imagine the situation as best you can. For example, I do have an idea of what my mother looks like even when I am not looking at her or a picture of her. Usually, as you continue to practice, you will feel more comfortable with imaging.

Other people find their images are so vivid it is almost as if

they are watching a videotape. This is a particular gift or apti-
tude. Several times people have become frightened because
their images were so realistic they thought they might have
been hallucinating. If you have this gift, just enjoy it.

In the various prayer experiences I ask you to image God,
your Higher Power, holding you or touching you in some way.
If someone wounded you so much that you don't trust touch,
build up to visualizing yourself in the arms of your Higher
Power. In *The Little Prince* by Antoine de Saint-Exupéry, the
fox tells the Little Prince that he must tame the fox if they are to
play together. The fox states that "to tame" means "to establish
ties," and this must be done slowly. We also need to take the
time to establish ties with God. We are the ones who need to be
tamed. For instance, you may want to begin by imagining your
Higher Power being with you and simply doing what you want
to do. That may be as simple and basic as sitting and talking
without having to worry about being hurt. After you feel comfortable with that experience, you may then want your Higher
Power to briefly touch you in some way. This could be a pat on
the shoulder or another gentle touch. From here you could
progress to holding hands with your Higher Power. When you
are comfortable with holding hands, see your Higher Power
with an arm around your shoulder. You might then be ready for
a hug. Increase the time of the hug until you are able to be held
by your Higher Power for longer periods of time.

Take your time with this experience. Avoid the trap of
getting angry or frustrated with yourself because you are uncomfortable with your Higher Power. Remember, someone
may have deeply wounded you. You are only protecting yourself when you avoid touch. Take time to build up that trust and
be comfortable. Your Higher Power will not get impatient and
leave you. God will always be there. You just need time with

your Higher Power for you to believe this. Take the time. You are worth it.

Let us now go through the basic prayer experience.

RELAXATION PRAYER

Get into a comfortable position. Close your eyes and take some deep breaths. Imagine your Higher Power's love surrounding you in some color. Imagine any uncomfortable feelings inside you in another color. Inhale deeply and slowly. See the color representing your Higher Power's love enter you. When you exhale see the color that represents any uncomfortable feelings leave you. Each time you inhale visualize your Higher Power's love filling you. Each time you exhale see the uncomfortable feelings leave you. As you continue to inhale and exhale watch your Higher Power's love push out your uncomfortable feelings. Give those feelings permission to leave you, at least temporarily. As you inhale see the color of your Higher Power's love fill your head. As love fills your head allow the muscles in your head to relax and allow God's love to fill you. As you continue to breathe in the color of love, see love travel down your neck lengthening and relaxing those muscles. Just allow the love to fill you and relax you. Love continues down into your shoulders bringing warmth and relaxation. Allow the muscles of your shoulders to lengthen and relax. If your shoulders are hunched up, allow them to drop. See love progress down into your arms. Just see the love flow from the top of your arms down into your hands and fingers. Allow your arms to rest where they are. As you relax your arms will grow heavy. See the love continue down your back like warm water bringing warmth and relaxation to those muscles. As you continue to breathe deeply the love fills your chest bringing relax-

ation to all the muscles and organs in your chest. Love continues into your abdominal area relaxing all the muscles and organs
there. Allow your muscles and organs, especially your intes-
tines, to let go and relax. Breathing in deeply, see the love continue into your pelvic area bringing warmth and relaxation.
Love progresses into your thighs . . . your knees . . . your shins
and calves . . . and into your feet and toes. All the muscles are
letting go and relaxing. One more time breathe in deeply and
watch as the color representing the love of your Higher Power
circulates within you. For a few moments, allow yourself to rest
in this love. Know that love is within you.

SAFE PLACE

After you have relaxed form an image in your mind of a
place outside that will be your safe place. Your safe place is
where you and your Higher Power, God, can talk, and share,
and be. In this place anything you feel and experience will lead
to healing, to wholeness. Form an image of your safe place.
What is there? What kinds of plants, trees or flowers are there?
What do you see? What does the air smell like? Can you feel
the sun against your skin? What can you hear? Are there birds
or insects in your safe place? Is there water nearby? What does
it feel like and sound like when you walk? Walk around your
safe place and become comfortable with it.

Your safe place is for you and your Higher Power. Your
Higher Power comes to you, sees you and smiles. Your Higher
Power hugs you, calls you by name and says "I love you. I love
you more than you could ever know." Rest in the arms of your
Higher Power. Either go walking or sit and talk with your
Higher Power. Tell your Higher Power whatever is on your
mind and in your heart. Listen. What is the response? When
you have finished your conversation, very gently come back to
your room. You may need to wiggle your fingers and toes to

help you come back to the present moment. You may want to record images, thoughts and feelings in your journal.

FURTHER EXPERIENCES

After the discussion for each Step there are suggestions for further prayer and meditation experiences. Most of the imaging experiences will have you begin in your safe place. It is a good idea to begin your meditation and prayer experiences with some type of relaxation prayer. As you relax you lower your defenses and become more open to the healing potential in these meditation exercises. As you practice the relaxation prayer you will discover that gradually it will take less time for you to relax. Many people have said they can begin to relax when they imagine the color of God's love. Others relax when they imagine their safe place.

2

POWER AND POWERLESSNESS

When someone has been emotionally or physically battered all their lives because of their gender, race, socioeconomic class, religion, sexual orientation or for any other reason, the last thing they need is to begin a program that tells them they are powerless. They know they are powerless. They don't need to continue affirming their sense of powerlessness. If the 12-Steps is so great, why does it affirm powerlessness?

The answer to this question revolves around the concept of power. What is power? Where does it come from? If the 12-Steps affirms powerlessness, does that mean power is bad? This chapter will address some theoretical points about power, and discuss how the AA interpretation of powerlessness developed.

Those who founded Alcoholics Anonymous used principles which worked for them. Every program that is established comes from the lived experiences of one or more people. The experiences of the founders brought them to understand certain concepts—for instance "powerlessness" in the 12-Step program—in a particular manner. The lived experiences of those who follow, however, may not bring the same understanding of those concepts.

The 12-Steps of Alcoholics Anonymous was begun by two men who had experienced a great deal of personal power in their lives before alcoholism almost killed them. Bill states in his story "I, who had thought so well of myself and my abilities, of my capacity to surmount obstacles, was cornered at last (by the effects of alcoholism)."[1] Both founders had been successful professional men. Bill had come home from World War I a victor and later became a successful businessman; Dr. Bob had been a successful physician.

Bill W. and Dr. Bob's recovery, and the recovery of millions, consisted in believing they were powerless over alcohol. These men, who had previously accomplished a great deal in their lives, had absolutely no power to be able to drink without drinking themselves into unconsciousness. A liquid which ninety percent of the population could drink on occasion had the power to kill them. These once powerful men had to not only convince themselves they were powerless, but they had to believe it. They had to do this in order to live!

After they knew they were powerless over alcohol they discovered their Higher Power, who many of us call God. They had a spiritual experience. Their lives were turned around. "The central fact of our lives today is the absolute certainty that our Creator has entered into our hearts and lives in a way that is indeed miraculous. [Our Creator] has commenced to accomplish those things for us which we could never do ourselves."[2] Their alcoholism was not cured, but they no longer had the desire to drink. God was now a part of their lives. God filled the hole in their lives and they became whole. They discovered their personal power again. The difference was that, this time, they knew the source of their power was the Higher Power, God.

Bill W. and Dr. Bob's story has been repeated time and time again in different forms. In the back of the Big Book, *Alcoholics Anonymous,* you will find more than forty stories to give you hope and inspiration. In all the stories the individuals "Give up power to get power." What does this mean?

A clue to the meaning of the above slogan can be found in the Big Book. "The first requirement is that we be convinced that any life run on self-will can hardly be a success. On that basis we are almost always in collusion with something or somebody, even though our motives are good."[3] Self-will is the key to the AA notion of powerlessness. When the 12-Steps state that we must admit our powerlessness, we can interpret that to mean that we must admit we can no longer run our lives alone, through our own self-will. We need help.

When those of us who are alcoholics admit we are powerless over alcohol, we mean that we are powerless to change what alcohol does to us through our own self-will. We cannot ever drink again if we want to stay sober. We are powerless over alcohol. To gain power over our craving for alcohol we have to give up our self-will and rely upon God, our Higher Power.

The power we gain when we give up our self-will was always present within us. How is that so? Power is part of our humanity, just as the capacity to love is part of our humanity. We were given both gifts by our Creator. Just as there are many of us who are not able to love or accept love, there are those of us who abuse power and hurt others. Each of us has the capacity to love or to hate (opposites) and to use power to build up or to destroy (opposites). All of us have seen or experienced at one time or another the power of love as well as the power of hate.

Many of us began investigating 12-Step programs because we had been the victims of the abuse of power. Each of us who came from a dysfunctional family came from a situation in which power was abused. Parents have tremendous power. Parents can call their children to growth through the words they use ("I'm so proud of you," "You really show much effort in what you are doing," "When you smile like that I feel warm all over") and their actions (hugs, listening). The destructive use of power is when a parent physically, sexually or emotionally

("You're so stupid," "I wish you had never been born") abuses. Look into your own hearts. How did your parents' use of power affect you? How has your use of power affected your children?

Each one of you who has experienced abusive power has experienced the type of power the 12-Steps calls us to give up. When we use power to get someone to do something we want in a way which is abusive we are using our own self-will. We are being coercive. Abusive power brings pain and alienates people from each other. Using power in an abusive manner hardens the spirit of individuals, rendering them incapable of tender, honest, intimate relationships. Each time we use power in an abusive manner we not only hurt others, but also harm ourselves. People who rely on abusive power are insecure within themselves. They need external forces, such as bodyguards, violence or money, to help them feel secure. Such insecure, but worldly-powerful people, try to acquire "love" through money, threats or physical force to keep people in line. What they get is not love or respect, but resentment and anger. Self-confidence which derives from this type of power is not self-confidence at all, but confidence in the tool used to get what is wanted.

We hear of murders so often that they hardly affect us unless it involves someone we know, have heard of, or a child. Hate crimes are occurring more frequently. Nazi swastikas are appearing on synagogues, people are being killed because of their sexual orientation, and sex crimes of all kinds have increased. There are abuses of power that never make the news. Someone belittles or degrades another for their own personal gain. Words are said that ruin someone's reputation or rupture relationships. We can see abusive power almost everywhere if we open our eyes and look.

Anytime we try to control or manipulate someone into doing something we want them to do for our own personal gain, we are abusing power. This is the kind of power that we want to get rid of. If this is the only way we know how to use power, then we want to become powerless. Only by ridding ourselves of this kind of power can we acquire the power that brings peace and healing, God's power.

We know we are seeing power exercised when we see abusive power, but what about people who seem totally ineffective in their lives? How can we say they have power?

In a land far away and a time long ago, the soil was dry and parched. There was no water for miles around. Every once in a while it rained for a few minutes. Other than that everything was dry. One day the earth shook so furiously that the land was rearranged. Where there were plains there were now valleys and hills. Most remarkable, however, was a crack in the earth that appeared and from which fresh spring water came forth. The land was continually watered. There were now plants and flowers. Animals came and drank from the spring.

In this land the water had always been there. No one could see it because there was no opening for the water to escape. Ineffectual people are not that way because they have no power, but because they have not learned to tap the source of their power. Once individuals connect with the source of power, they will discover their own personal power.

There is no one way that the discovery of God's power occurs for everyone. What does happen is that we begin to look somewhere other than at ourselves for power. We begin to discover our spiritual selves. We become aware of that part of us which yearns to be connected to other people and to a Power greater than ourselves. We discover God.

When we discover God within us, who is the source of power, we find our personal power. Our personal power, which is part of our spiritual selves, was always there. We just didn't know it. We couldn't use our personal power if we weren't aware of it. Now that we have discovered the God within, the source of our personal power, we can be truly self-confident. We no longer need rely on people or things outside of ourselves to "make" us feel powerful.

As I've listened to the stories of people's lives I've discovered that almost all have had some sense of personal power at some time. This may have happened when they were very young or at a time of accomplishment. Some were not aware of their power because they were made to feel that this was wrong. Maybe they were told they shouldn't be proud. If our personal power is not affirmed it cannot develop. If we are continually abused and oppressed, our personal power is stunted. We feel ineffective and inferior. We have no sense of who we are, of our giftedness. We have little or no sense of self-worth.

Our lack of self-worth leads us to do one of two things with our personal power. One way is to bury our power. We may not want to become like those who have caused harm, or we may have believed that since others had such power over us there is no way we ourselves could have power. Others of us exhibit grandiosity in our words and actions, which could cause us to exercise power in an abusive manner.

How do we find our personal power or how do we keep from exercising power in a destructive manner? The answer to both questions is the same: Find God, who is the source of your power. If we form a relationship with God we will be connected to the source of power. We will remain centered and stable. When we are not connected with God, our power source, we will not be centered and will tend to abuse power.

Step 1 affirms powerlessness over alcohol. Step Spirit affirms powerlessness over people, places and things. We cannot control people, events or objects through our own self-will. The key to understanding powerlessness in the context of the 12-Steps is to realize the paradox of how limited our power is, but, simultaneously, how our personal power can effect change in ourselves and bring healing to others.

3

STEP 1

We admitted that we were powerless over alcohol (people, places and things) and our lives had become unmanageable.

Just as every journey begins with a single step, the 12-Step program begins with Step 1. Contained within Step 1 are two key concepts: 1) we are powerless over alcohol, drugs, people, places and things, and 2) our lives are unmanageable. For us to work Step 1 we will need to admit that each concept contained in Step 1 is a part of our lives. As we come to believe the implications of Step 1 we will discover changes in the emotional, behavioral, and spiritual aspects of our lives. These changes come neither easily nor immediately. We must work, and work hard, at understanding and incorporating into our lives what Step 1 requires. Understanding is only one element in bringing about change within ourselves. To change we must first make a decision to change, and then act upon that decision.

Step 1 is the foundation of all the Steps. Without this foundation in place we will have a difficult, if not impossible, time with each succeeding Step. None of us can attain true sobriety, be it from chemicals, unhealthy relationships, or other compulsions without having Step 1 deeply ingrained into our very souls.

The first idea we need to incorporate into our lives is the idea of "powerlessness." The very idea that we are powerless over people, places and things is an alien concept to many of us, especially men, in our North American culture. We in the United States grew up with the notion that we could do anything we wanted if we put our minds to it. How often have you heard: "Pull yourself up by your bootstraps," "Where there is a will there is a way," and other such slogans. There is even "God helps those who help themselves," which, by the way, is not found in the Bible, but was popularized by Benjamin Franklin. Being powerless is almost an un-American idea.

However, the truth of the matter is that we, alone, always were powerless. The reason we as individuals and as a country have accomplished so much is not because of our individual selves, but because God within us has given us many gifts enabling us to accomplish all we have accomplished.

But that is not all. Even in seemingly simple individual accomplishments we have needed other people as well as God. Every person who has touched our lives, both positively and negatively, has brought us to where we are today in our personal development. Even when we are in touch with God's power within us, we are not so full of power that we do not need other people. Without other people we would not have the food we eat, the clothes we wear, the knowledge we've gained, or the love we've given and received. Each of us is interdependent with others for our survival.

The personal power we have is given to us by our Higher Power, God. We become truly powerful only when we claim our God-given power and use it according to our God-given gifts and talents. When we believe we are the source of our own power we have little room for a Power greater than ourselves. In effect, we have established ourselves as gods. Our self-appointed "god" status brings about a destructive pride producing behaviors which alienate and isolate us from others.

There are those of us who are not in touch with our God-given power. We resort to drugs, alcohol, money, sex or violence to make us feel powerful. Some of us believe another person contains the power we need to make us whole. We believe these objects or people are what give us value. When we do this we make something or someone else our god. Eventually, these material, finite things will fail us in some way. We will begin to discover, much to our horror, that what we believed gave us power was, instead, a false sense of power. Our misconceptions so filled us we could not touch the Power within us, who is the source of all power.

Without a belief in a Higher Power we fight hard to keep the illusion that our addiction or compulsion is power. We try to manipulate and control everything and everyone around us to keep our false belief. Control of others becomes the major attitude of those of us struggling with addictions and compulsions. We do whatever is necessary to obtain our drug or continue our compulsion. This requires attempts to control others. When we operate from control we mistakenly believe we ourselves are keeping everything in order, that our lives are being held together by our own efforts and our own will. We have this false belief that our power comes from ourselves and, by self-will, we can keep our lives or the lives of others on track.

But we can't. Things are falling apart around us. We are either always drunk or high, or we are trying to keep someone else from being drunk or high, or we're trying to get someone else to do something we think she or he should be doing. Despite all the energy and all the effort we expend in controlling the various aspects of our lives and the lives of others, things are still crumbling around us. We feel empty inside, disconnected. "If only I could try a little harder" or "If only I can do this one thing everything will be fine." Those are the slogans by which we live our lives. As things get worse we say them more often. We try one strategy and then another, believing and hoping the very next one will be the answer. But it isn't.

We are powerless to control anyone and anything except ourselves; and there are even things about ourselves we cannot control. If we are an addict we are powerless over drugs and alcohol. Those of us in relationships with addicts are powerless over the addict. All of us are powerless to make anyone be, feel, and do exactly what we want. We have very limited control over what happens in the world at large. More often than not we have no control over when the tire will go flat, when the refrigerator will go out, when the postal service actually delivers its next day's mail, or when the economy takes a downturn. We have no control over the weather, insurance rates, and very limited control over how the government spends our money. We are powerless over people, places and things.

Nothing we are presently doing is the answer to all our woes or we wouldn't be in this fix. What is happening is beyond our own capabilities to change. There is no way any one of us can repair the chaos in our lives without help. If we can't bring order out of our own chaos how can we even presume to think we can fix the lives of others?

Admitting we are powerless over people, places and things, and that our lives have become unmanageable, can be one of the most difficult, yet one of the most freeing, admissions of our lives. It is usually beyond our comprehension that admitting powerlessness and unmanageability will help us find peace. For many, if not most of us, this admission implies we have given up or we are defeated. However, this is exactly what the First Step is asking us to do: admit defeat. BUT, we are only admitting defeat in relation to our way of doing things.

The First Step is not asking us to give up on life but to try something new. What we have been doing up to this point hasn't worked. Many of us are in indescribable pain. We probably have lost our identity by doing things the way we always have. What have we to lose if we try something new?

Admitting we are powerless over people, places and things is more than an intellectual assent. Step 1 requires knowing to the very depth of our being that we cannot control our own and others' addictions and compulsions. What emotions come from that revelation! Because we believe we are powerless over people, places and things, fear, sadness and anger often surface. We feel fearful because we feel unprotected. Where will our protection come from? Who will help us?

Sadness and anger are both emotions found in grieving. When we realize we are powerless over so much that affects our lives we begin to grieve for the loss of what we believed was power but was, in reality, only an illusion. That illusion had protected us, served us, or so we thought, for some time. We may become sad, depressed or fearful because the power, which we never actually had, is gone. We may become angry because we now have to face the reality that all our efforts at controlling ourselves or someone else have been futile.

When we accept the knowledge of our powerlessness over people, places and things some amazing changes take place within us. We become vulnerable, and that can be very frightening! Many of us believe being "vulnerable" means only that we can be hurt. When our defenses are down, when we are vulnerable, someone can do or say something that could hurt us. We fear being hurt in this manner. Vulnerability, however, has another side. Vulnerability also means we are open to the love of God and others, and we are open to change.

If we do not allow ourselves to be vulnerable we cannot love or be loved to the extent we are capable of. Unless we allow ourselves to risk being vulnerable we cannot change our unhealthy behaviors and thought processes. Being *in*vulnerable may protect us from pain, but it also keeps us from experiencing joy. The hardness that comes from protecting ourselves from feeling, from hurting, also repels love, thus keeping us rigid and immobile.

Admitting our powerlessness frees us to allow the One who is Power to become active in our lives. We become more open to new ways of doing things as we allow God to love us and teach us how to give and receive love. We also begin to accept people and situations as they are. As we realize we aren't in control, but God is in control, we are more able to detach from people and situations that are unhealthy for us, and accept these the way they are. This doesn't mean we quit caring. We care, but we don't allow the situation to determine our thoughts, actions and feelings. We will discover, as our detachment and acceptance deepens, that we have more emotional energy to spend on ourselves and the activities we would like to do.

The emotional component of Step 1 is getting in touch with our powerlessness over people, places and things. The behavioral response to Step 1 is letting go of control. Not controlling means we do not try to manage anyone's life in any way. Not controlling means we allow other people to be responsible for their lives. Not controlling means we focus on ourselves and not on other people. We begin to listen to others and, on occasion, try things their way. No longer are we rigidly wedded to the notion that our way is the only correct way. Not controlling means letting go and going with the flow.

At first we may find it difficult to see the ways in which we control. Our methods of control, both subtle and blatant, have become so ingrained we believe they are part of us. Often we mistake control for caring. To discover the ways we control we need group support and feedback. As we listen to others who are farther along in their journey than we are, we will hear about ways in which they have controlled. From this information we can learn how we control. We also need the group to let us know we are not terrible people because we control. We need people to help us realize that control is part of the dysfunction, not part of us. We need people in our lives to demonstrate ways to relate to people without attempting to force them to be who we want them to be.

As we come to know others in our support group we will meet people who have something within them we want—serenity. There is no way we will find serenity until we begin to admit we are powerless by ourselves and that we are not in control. Our Higher Power cannot enter our lives unless we give up control; there isn't any room. Faith and control are mutually exclusive. When we truly admit powerlessness over people, places and things there is a radical change within our spiritual centers. As we release control by admitting powerlessness, we begin to open our minds, hearts, and spirits to the love of our Higher Power and to the goodness of our companion human beings.

Getting in touch with our powerlessness is very scary. Frequently we are left with a helpless feeling. We ask the questions: "If I am powerless then is there no hope?" "Who can fix this mess?" When we come to these questions we are ready for Step 2. Step 2 begins to show us where both hope and power reside.

ESPECIALLY FOR WOMEN

Through my personal experiences and my work I have found the interpretation of Step 1, and all the Steps, can be different for women. Many women are aware they grew up in an oppressive atmosphere. Their talents were not allowed to develop, or even were denied, because they were female. I have worked with many women who felt inferior to their brothers because their family catered to the development of the male members of the family and ignored the female. The young girl was required to stay behind and clean while the boy went fishing with the men. In many cases the females of the family were required, at a young age, to satisfy the sexual wants of the male family members.

Almost all coeducational school systems are established in such a way that male leadership is developed and female leadership denied. Male sports are emphasized and receive most of the funding and publicity. The male is looked upon as a potential leader and the female is seen as a potential helper of the male.

In society women face sexual harassment, rape, the glass ceiling inhibiting advancement and non-recognition of their gifts and talents. Advertising continually objectifies women as sexual objects in order to sell automobiles, shaving cream, clothes, and so forth. The message communicated is that to be truly feminine a woman must be at least 5'7" tall, slim, very attractive, no older than the mid-twenties, white and preferably blond. Television and movies frequently place women as the powerless victims of crimes, who can only be saved by the more powerful male.

Many women who come to a 12-Step group in hopes of putting their lives back together are further demoralized when reading Step 1. "Powerless," they say, "of course I'm powerless. I've always been powerless. I'm tired of being powerless." As they say this they may also feel somewhere within themselves that they want power, but not the power that destroys.

Those of you who already feel you are powerless will have an easier time grasping the concepts of Step 1 than those of you who don't. You may be well aware that lack of personal power results in feeling ineffectual. You may be very angry about this powerlessness. This anger is a sign that you have already begun grieving for your lack of power. Rejoice that you are angry! Healing has begun because grieving has begun.

The question remains: Where is the source of our power, the power to bring good, not to destroy? The answer: Where it has always been—within each one of us. The source of power is the God within. Step 2 will begin to show you how to connect with the source.

PRAYER EXPERIENCES

1. Do the relaxation prayer outlined in the first chapter. After you feel relaxed and peaceful go to your safe place. Spend some time with your Higher Power. Tell your Higher Power how you feel about being powerless over people, places and things. Express all your feelings, be they anger, despair, sadness, hope or fear. Listen to what your Higher Power says to you. What feelings are you having while you talk to your Higher Power in this manner? After you end the meditation you may want to record your experiences in your journal.

2. Begin this prayer with the relaxation prayer to help you connect with your Higher Power. Write a conversation between you and God about your feelings of powerlessness over people, places and things just as if you were writing a script for a play. You may want to write several conversations over time as you grapple with the concept of powerlessness. Do not be afraid of any feelings that come forth in your journal writing. Many people become frightened and ashamed because they find they are angry with God. There is nothing wrong with being angry with God. God is the one Being who will neither shame you into believing anger is wrong, nor turn away from you when you are angry. One individual related how her feelings of closeness to God increased when she could be angry with God and not worry about being abandoned. Here was one Being with whom she could be totally honest about her feelings. How freeing!

3. This is your own First-Step prayer you can pray every day. In this prayer write about your powerlessness over people,

places and things and what it means to you. Write whatever it is you need to remind yourself of your powerlessness over many of life's situations. Once you have written your prayer put it where you will pray it every day—in a meditation book, on your bathroom mirror.

4

STEP 2

Came to believe that a Power greater than ourselves could restore us to sanity.

Our Step 1 admission of powerlessness over people, places and things removes our false belief that we are the one in control of everything. Once we realize we are not in control we have room in our lives for the One who is in control. Yet, being in touch with our powerlessness may also leave us feeling exposed and unprotected. If we do not have power in our lives, who does? If we do not have power, how are we going to get ourselves out of the mess in which we believe we are deeply mired? If we have no control over things, who does? These questions move us from acknowledging our powerlessness over people, places and things to the discovery of the One with all the power, God, our Higher Power.

All too frequently some people reach this Step and become scared. They believe they can't work this Step because they don't want to have anything to do with God. The reasons people want to avoid God are many. Perhaps, as a child, they learned about a punishing, judging God. Religion may have been stuffed down their throats all their lives. Perhaps someone abused them in some way in the name of God or religion. It could be they were never introduced to a loving God. Then again, maybe God was important to them at one time and they either drifted away or were filled with bitterness because they believed God had let them down in some way. If you are someone who fits into the descriptions of this paragraph Step 2 will introduce you, or reintroduce you, to your Higher Power.

Step 2 is not about religion. It is about spirituality. Spirituality is about that part within us that reaches for relationships beyond ourselves. Almost all of us have experienced our spiritual selves in some manner. Have you ever been struck with wonder and awe at the beauty of a sunset, or the majesty of mountains, or the innocence of a child? Have you ever experienced love or peace that seemed to pull you to some dimension beyond yourself? If you have, you, through your spiritual self, have been touched in some way by a Power greater than yourself. You became aware of something, someone greater than yourself. To continue the Steps you will begin to tap into your spiritual self and discover how to be more in touch with this Higher Power, the source of all power, who draws you beyond yourself into relationships with others, nature and God.

Many people involved in organized religion have a tendency to gloss over Step 2. They believe they already have this Step well in hand because they are going to church. If you are one of these folks, hang on. Spend some time in searching reflection on the following questions:

> Have you come to know God? Is God someone you can sit and chat with anytime you want? Do you have a peaceful sense of God's presence? Do you believe God loves and accepts you as an individual, just as you are, no matter what you might have done in the past? Is God so important to you that you would talk over decisions before you finalize them, just like you'd discuss things with a friend? Do you really believe you can trust God to do things better than

you can? Really look into your heart to answer these questions.

The above questions are about relationship. Step 2 is the beginning of a special relationship. When I ask people how their relationship is with their Higher Power I often get responses such as "My family went to church every Sunday when I was a kid and now I go to church most Sundays." Other times I hear, "I don't believe I need church to talk with God." Those responses don't answer the question I asked. The answers given are to an unasked question about how religious a person is. What is important to recovery is not how religious we are, what "church" activities we do to express our beliefs, but what our relationship with God is.

People frequently confuse religion, spirituality and God. All three are different but, hopefully, interrelated. Religion has to do with rituals, activities, rules and dogma that a particular group—Protestants, Catholics, Jews, Muslims—use in their worship of God. Unfortunately, just as some parents do not have a true relationship with their children, some people who participate in organized religion have little personal connection with God or their Higher Power. They are not in touch with their spirituality, that part of themselves that goes out to God, others and the world. These people may be what is called religious, but they are not spiritual. They do things that relate *to* God, but they themselves do not have a relationship *with* God.

Relationship with God means we allow ourselves to continually discover who God is for us. We are open to entering into the mystery of relationship with God. Questions we may investigate are: What role does God play in my life? Where does my concept of God come from? Am I able to communicate with God? Is God a loving force in my life? The answers to these questions and others come by being open to the possibility that our Higher Power, God, is much more than we could ever imagine. We will need to put aside our present perceptions of who or what God is and be open to the possibility of surprise in discovering who God is for us.

Frequently, people question the use of the term "Higher Power." They will say, "If you mean 'God' then just say 'God'!" As you read this material you will notice that "God" and "Higher Power" are used interchangeably. Alcoholics Anonymous uses the term "Higher Power" for good reason. If I say the word "God" or "Jesus," different thoughts, feelings and images come to mind according to past experiences. These images can be used either in a positive or a negative manner. The positive images can enhance one's relationship with God or Jesus and, therefore, ease the working of the 12-Steps. The negative images, however, could impede one from even beginning the Second Step, which would block recovery.

The term "Higher Power" is, for most people, a neutral term. Unless we grew up in a family that used this term with frequency, most of us have no preconceived notions of what "Higher Power" means. "God" may evoke images of an old man with a white beard, or a Being who watches us, ready to strike us with lightning bolts if we make one wrong move. The phrase "Higher Power" does not come laden with images. We are able to spend time discovering who our "Higher Power" is, what the characteristics of our "Higher Power" are, and what type of relationship we will have with our Higher Power.

To begin this adventure, do your best to put aside all negative preconceived ideas of God. Many of us have ideas of God as someone who loves us only if we are "good," or a God who is somewhere "out there" and not really interested or involved in our lives. Others of us view God as either male or female. There are many other images of God we might have. Try to put these aside for now. You may want to bring some of them back in an altered form at a later time. For the moment, try to put aside all images of God that bring up negative feelings in you.

Hold on to your positive images, but leave room for development.

The following may help you discover who your Higher Power is. Go somewhere where you can be quiet. Do the relaxation prayer. Quiet yourself. Ask your Higher Power to reveal her/himself to you. Then begin to list the emotional qualities you would like in a friend as well as the qualities you yourself would like to have. If you write "someone who loves me," define in behavioral terms what you mean by "love." Your list might include characteristics such as: trustworthy, faithful, caring and accepting. You may want to work on this list over a period of days or weeks.

Once you have the beginnings of a list of characteristics of your Higher Power, begin to talk to this Higher Power. It's easier than you think. Just imagine your Higher Power sitting in the room with you. Each time you talk to your Higher Power be conscious that you are talking to someone who has the characteristics you have listed. For example, "accepting" is on my list of characteristics of my Higher Power. When I pray, which is "talking to God," I am conscious that God is accepting me as I am and not asking me to be someone else. Remember, your Higher Power has unconditional positive regard for you. This is one relationship where all you have to do is be honest. God will not leave you or get bored.

Relationships are formed by spending time with someone, by talking and by listening. Your relationship with your Higher Power will be no different. Give yourself time and space to allow your relationship to grow gradually. Rarely do people have a "lightning bolt" type of spiritual experience. Usually, over time, we come to realize we are feeling more serene, more at peace, more connected. The key to spiritual awakening and growth is to spend time developing our spiritual side. (For additional suggestions on ways to spend time with your Higher Power refer to Step 11.)

People frequently ask questions about the phrase "restore us to sanity." What does that mean? One simple definition of insanity is "doing the same thing repeatedly expecting different results." For instance trying to get from Houston to Chicago by going west isn't at all efficient unless you really did want to spend time in California. If we keep going in the wrong direction when trying to get to a particular place we need to try something different—like a different direction.

For an addict, an example of insane behavior would be using the drug to feel less lonely, but feeling even more lonely and ashamed after using than before using. The addict keeps drugging thinking, "This time I will feel better," but, instead, feels worse. For someone in relationship with an alcoholic, insane behavior would be continually pouring out all the liquor, with either the silent treatment or rage thrown in for good measure, expecting our significant other to quit drinking. It doesn't work. Insanity may also include the expectations and hopes someone will change, even when they have had the same behaviors for years, with no sign of willingness or desire to change. Insanity is repeatedly doing these things with the same results and not trying something new, but expecting something new to happen.

Working the Steps is something new. Letting go of control is something new. Accepting powerlessness is something new. Really believing there is a Power greater than ourselves who can restore us to sanity is something new. All it takes is a willingness to try these Steps and a willingness to trust. At the very least, be willing to be willing to trust.

Trust. What a tremendous word. One thing we haven't done in the midst of our addiction or compulsion is to trust, to let go. We haven't trusted others. We haven't trusted God. We haven't even trusted ourselves. This Step is asking us to begin trusting. We begin trusting in slow, often painful, degrees. When we spend time with our Higher Power during our periods of prayer and meditation we are beginning to trust. As we use the meditation exercises in this book we will begin to trust. We must allow ourselves time to trust. We have been very wounded and it takes time to heal. As long as we are working the 12-Step program, doing our prayer and meditation and working on our recovery, we are doing what we need to be doing. Trust will gradually build within us.

ESPECIALLY FOR WOMEN

When examining our concept of God it might be helpful to realize that almost everything, if not everything, we know about the Judeo-Christian concept of God comes from men. The Judeo-Christian scriptures were written by men. Most theologians, those who study God issues, are men or women who have not yet investigated the feminine dimension of God and spirituality.

Take a risk in investigating who God is to you. If you have always imaged God as male, try imaging God as female. Assign to your female image of God all the characteristics you want her to have. Remember that your female God is the Higher Power, All-Powerful. Feel what it is like to have a female Higher Power when you have always been told God is male. Does your female image feel comfortable or uncomfortable? Does it bring you peace or fear? Why? If you can identify with the image of a female God, what do you think that will do to your own self-image as woman?

There is nothing wrong or sinful in thinking of God as feminine. God is neither male nor female. God is Love itself and love has no gender. Although God is infinite, we human beings attempt to place God within our own finite structure. If imagining God as feminine and calling God "Mother" is healing for you, then do so. What is important is forming our own relationship with God.

PRAYER EXPERIENCES

1. Pray the relaxation prayer and go to your safe place. Spend some time seeing yourself in the arms of your Higher Power. During different prayer times imagine yourself at various ages. For example, see yourself as a baby and God holding you. Another time see yourself as a four-year-old or a teenager. Have your Higher Power play with you or hold you or speak to you the way you would like. Stay with the age you have chosen until you feel ready to move to a different age. You will automatically be choosing those times in which you needed more nurturing than you received.

2. While in your safe place, image God as Father if you need a father's love, or God as Mother if you need a mother's love. Be whatever age you need to be during this prayer.

3. Take with you your list of qualities you would like your Higher Power to have. Do the relaxation prayer and go into your safe place. Get in touch with how it feels to be in the presence of someone with one or more of the qualities you have on your list. Image yourself with your Higher Power who has those qualities most important to you. Share with your Higher Power whatever is in your heart.

4. We often have nicknames for those close to us. As you begin to feel connected with your Higher Power, choose a nickname, a term of endearment, for your Higher Power. Use that name in prayer.

5

STEP 3

Made a decision to turn our wills and our lives over to the care of God as we understood him (her).

In beginning Step 2 we take what we have learned in the first two Steps and travel farther in our journey. We progress from acknowledgment of a Higher Power to further discovering who this Higher Power is for us as individuals. Only after we have completed the last phase of Step 3, "... God as we understood him (her)," can we begin the decision part of this Step.

In Step 2 we began to give intellectual assent to the concept of a Higher Power and to come to an understanding of God, our Higher Power, for ourselves. Our own understanding of God for us is critical for the working of Step 3. We will turn our wills and our lives over to the care of someone we trust and with whom we are comfortable. We will build a barrier between someone we don't trust or don't understand. There will usually be a wall between ourselves and God if our concept of God is not our own. Remember, if you have never formed your idea of God or what God is like, your concept of your Higher Power is just beginning. Your understanding of God is going to deepen, and maybe even change, as you grow and develop spiritually in relationship to your Higher Power.

For example, a child's understanding of God grows and develops over time. Children frequently think of God as a man somewhere "out there" who has either a white beard or a long robe or both. Gradually the child may come to see God as a type of magician or Santa Claus who delivers when asked. As time progresses and the relationship grows the child will eventually talk to his or her God as a friend. Unfortunately, for most human beings, our spiritual relationship with God doesn't progress much beyond viewing God as Santa Claus. We seem to spend our prayer time asking God to give us things or to cause things to happen.

Many people believe God loves them only if their prayers are answered the way they want. If we reflect upon the attitude of "we ask and God delivers if he/she cares," attempts on our part to manipulate God can be detected. We may develop the mindset that if we ask in just the right way, with the correct words, or often enough, God will grant us what we want. This is a form of manipulation we frequently use on those around us. We do not need to manipulate God, even if we could, into doing good for us. Our Higher Power has unconditional positive regard for us and wants only our good.

The relationship we are seeking with our Higher Power is based on care and concern, and not upon what we can receive. This may be a very different type of relationship than we are accustomed to. So often those of us who are addicted or are involved in some type of compulsion do not know what it is like to be in a relationship where a payoff isn't expected. Frequently we will do something for someone, expecting, in some part of ourselves, that the individual will respond in a particular manner. For example, many people who write letters expect one in return. If the individual does not receive a return letter, another letter is not sent. This is the pattern of many of our relationships. How different the relationship in which one writes the letter simply to share her or himself with another person, whether or not the other individual writes back.

The purpose in our establishing a relationship with God is not to get things, but simply to be in relationship with God. We do receive blessings and gifts when we place our trust in God. These gifts, peace and serenity among them, are not the primary reason we enter into relationship with God. They are the beautiful by-products of our time well spent.

Caught in our own addiction, or the addiction of someone else, frequently places us on a similar spiritual developmental plane as a child. How do we grow spiritually? If you have already worked Steps 1 and 2, you have already begun to grow. Using the prayer experiences after each Step, and following a program similar to the one outlined in the chapter on Step 11, will place you well on the road to spiritual growth. Like any journey, our spiritual journey is filled with pleasant and unpleasant surprises.

The Steps are not asking us to have someone's "perfect" notion of relationship with our Higher Power. The Steps are about our own individual relationship with our Higher Power as we ourselves understand him or her. As each of us works the program each of us will grow, at our own pace, in our own spiritual awareness and in our own individual relationship with our Higher Power. We listen to what others say about their understanding of God, but we form our own understanding.

Now that we are beginning to form our own understanding of our Higher Power we can look at the other dynamics of Step 3, "Made a decision to turn our wills and our lives over to the care of God. . . ." When we come to this first part of Step 3 we realize how far we have come in our working the Steps. We have already realized we are powerless over people, places and things and we have come to believe there is a Higher Power. This is a long way from the person who believed he or she was totally in control of his or her life and had to do everything alone. With Step 3 we make a conscious decision to turn everything over to the care of God. We decide to let someone else handle everything we have already made a mess of—and even those things we have done well.

This decision is not made just once in our lives. Often, it is a decision we make several times a day. For me this decision happens every day when things are going well, and about every minute when things are rough. When things are not going well in my life I have a tendency to revert to my old behavior of control. I become impatient and think I can do a better job than God. (Wow! What turmoil I have manufactured when I have done that!) A friend of mine called this particular pattern playing volleyball with God—"Here, you take it. No, I'll take it back." We are so used to playing by our own rules, with our own ball, under our own power that we don't know how to give something over to God. Just like playing volleyball, we practice and we practice and we practice. Each time we get better. As our relationship with our Higher Power grows we become healthier. Eventually we have peace and serenity because we let the ball stay in God's court.

Of course, there is another part to this decision. We do have to turn things over to God. This reminds me of a riddle I heard somewhere. "There were three frogs on a lily pad and two of them decided to jump. How many were left on the lily pad?" The answer—"Three, the two that had decided to jump hadn't done it yet." In our addiction and compulsion we are like those two frogs. We've made the decision but new behaviors are scary, so we don't jump. In Step 3 we take a deep breath, say a short prayer, then jump. Our Higher Power is there to catch us.

Remember, we are turning things over to the care of God. "Care." That word has such gentle connotations for me. There is protection, there is concern, there is support when I think of "care." I am turning my will and my life to someone, my Higher Power, who gives protection, concern, support—care. Love comes into the word "care." When I care for someone I have feelings of love, positive regard, for that person. When I turn my life over to the care of God I believe God has love for me. Since the word "love" has been overused, the impact of its meaning is often lost; therefore, I believe my Higher Power has unconditional positive regard for me. When I remember that, I don't mind turning things over to my Higher Power.

The problem with turning things over is that we so often have a difficult time turning over our expectations of how we want God to handle the problem. Our human tendency is to give God the problem with all the instructions, including a timetable. That is not turning the problem over to God. When we turn the problem over to God we also turn over our expectations and timetable. We tell God to handle the problem in the way God sees fit.

When we turn our problem over we are again admitting our powerlessness over people, places and things. We are again relinquishing control. We may have to turn the same problem over many times, with the prayer that God will help us not to take it back, but leave it with God. Each time we are able to give part of our lives to God, we connect with God within us. As we relinquish control to God we actually find we have greater control. Things don't seem as unmanageable as long as we leave things in God's hands.

As situations in our lives become more manageable we feel a greater sense of personal power, of self-confidence. We have grown spiritually to the point where we realize with God we can do anything. God is the source of power and God is within us. All we need to do is tap into the "Power Source" and use our new-found personal power with love and care.

These first three Steps require us to work on our internal self—our thoughts and attitudes. As we work these Steps we will notice a paradox. As we admit powerlessness we gain power; as we relinquish control, our life seems more in control. As we discontinue trying to control others, we discover our attempts at control were enslaving us. By turning things over to our Higher Power we gain a freedom from worry and anxiety that most of us have never experienced to any great extent.

Turning things over to the care of God does not mean we sit around and do nothing. The truth in the maxim, "God helps those who help themselves," is that we need to participate in working with God for our own well-being. A friend of mine says we need to do the leg work. We let God be the director, but we must be willing to follow direction. God isn't going to plop food in our laps if we are too lazy to get a job. God will help us cope with those times when we are caught in situations beyond our control. We need to keep reminding ourselves of God's faithfulness and readiness to help us. Pray often the following prayer by Reinhold Niebuhr:

> God, grant me serenity to accept the things I cannot change, courage to change the things I can and the wisdom to know the difference. Living one day at a time, enjoying one moment at a time, accepting hardship as a pathway to peace. Taking, as Jesus did, this sinful world as it is, not as I would have it. Trusting that You will make all things right if I surrender to Your will, so that I may be reasonably happy in this life and supremely happy with You forever in the next. Amen.

When we actually turn our lives and will over to the care of God we will notice a difference within us. Somehow we feel a lightness inside of ourselves we hadn't felt before. A burden is gone because we are allowing our Higher Power to carry that burden. We also notice a difference in our relationships. We no longer feel the same responsibility in "making" the relationship "work." We learn to turn our loved ones over to the care of

God. We begin to allow our loved ones to be themselves. Our relationships change at times because we have changed. As we achieve greater peace and serenity through these Steps we deepen our trust in our Higher Power. We become more open to God, ourselves and others.

Step 3 will continue our journey toward recovery. Our relationship with our Higher Power will continue to grow and develop as we become more comfortable with our own understanding of God. As our understanding of God increases we will be more able to trust God and to turn over our wills and our lives with trust. We continue to learn more about allowing our loved ones to be themselves, allowing ourselves to grow by relinquishing control, and discovering we can have peace and serenity.

ESPECIALLY FOR WOMEN

As we begin to grow more comfortable with our own image of our Higher Power, we frequently begin to notice that we, ourselves, feel powerful. As we turn things over to God we become more self-assured. This may be a new feeling for us. If raised in an environment where women were always degraded and considered inferior to men, you may doubt these new feelings. You may think you are wrong to feel this way.

Don't doubt! Hold onto those new feelings! You are beginning to experience what true personal power is. Your power is a gift from your Higher Power. This gift was given to you freely. You are precious. You are good. You are valuable. Now you are becoming aware of this.

The Higher Power who gave you these gifts is the One who is asking you to turn yourself over to her or him. Your Higher Power who cherishes you asks you to trust her or him. Before this time others may have told you they would take care of you, but didn't. Before this time others may have exerted a perverted form of power over you resulting in your being badly wounded. Now, by experiencing your own power given to you by God, you will learn to avoid people who use power in a destructive manner and gravitate toward those who use positive forms of power.

The stronger your connection to God, the more you will be able to trust God. The more you trust the more you will be able to turn your life and will over to God, and the stronger you will feel. You will feel more powerful. The paradox of admitting powerlessness, thereby discovering power, is experienced.

PRAYER EXPERIENCES

1. As usual, begin with the relaxation prayer and go into your safe place. Spend time, as needed, with your Higher Power. Talk to your Higher Power about what is going on with you right now. What is bothering you? Listen. Then imagine giving some symbol of yourself or your problem to your Higher Power. This represents your willingness to turn things over to God. See your Higher Power give a symbol of faithfulness to you. Place the symbol in your heart.

2. When talking to your Higher Power in your safe place, place the person you are worried about in the hands of your Higher Power. To symbolize this, take a picture of the person, or a piece of paper with the individual's name on it, and place it in a "safe place" that symbolizes your Higher Power's hands—then let it go.

3. Take a box (some use a shoe box) and slit a hole in the top. You might want to decorate the outside of the box. (One of my coworkers has "God Box" printed on the outside of her box.) Whenever you find yourself concerned about something

or someone, write that concern on a piece of paper. Say a prayer that turns the concern over to your Higher Power and place the paper in your box.

4. Say the Serenity Prayer every time you are struggling with something. Listen to the words as you say them.

5. When you feel especially anxious take out one of your meditation books and begin reading. Stick to it until you can calm down and "Let go, let God."

6

STEP 4

Made a searching and fearless moral inventory of ourselves.

In the first three Steps we began to address our delusion of being all-powerful by accepting that we are powerless over people, places and things. We then began to find our real power by establishing a relationship with our Higher Power. After we are able to turn things over to our Higher Power (Step 3) and get in touch with our personal power given to us by our Higher Power, we are ready to begin Step 4. Our Higher Power is the One who will give us the support and care we need to work our Fourth Step. Our Higher Power loves us totally, completely, and unconditionally, just the way we are. Our Higher Power loves us so much that she/he calls us to grow and develop into whole human beings who can freely love and be loved.

When people participate in Step studies, most of those who drop out, do so when Step 4 is reached. This is a very scary Step. In Step 4 we begin to look at ourselves with honesty. We write down all our faults and foibles. We read them. We acknowledge them. This process is a painful experience, and most of us want to avoid pain.

Pain is present in our emotional recovery just as it is present when we recover from surgery. People who are unable to feel physical pain are in great danger. They will not know they are hurt or ill. They can die of a ruptured appendix because they are unable to feel the pain from the rupture. Those who cannot experience emotional pain are also in great danger. They can be hard and withered inside and unable to experience the joys of life. They are dead within themselves.

The honesty required in Step 4 can open us to the gentle and powerful love of God if we continue to work our daily spiritual program. When we do a "fearless moral inventory" we face the truth about ourselves. We look at the barriers we have put around our hearts that prevent us from loving, even from loving ourselves. As we look at each item in our inventory, we begin to see the patterns of our thoughts, feelings and actions that keep us from being whole, healthy and happy people. It is normal to feel pain when we recall and list the events and attributes that have hurt ourselves as well as others. However, once we become aware of the negative behavior patterns and attitudes we will be able, with the help of our Higher Power, to change.

Step 4 is the beginning of a spiritual spring cleaning. When we speak of "spring cleaning" we usually mean the type of cleaning where we clean things we haven't cleaned in ages. We get behind everything and look for dirt in all the cracks and crevices. We also sort items in closets and drawers, throwing out what we don't need and keeping what we find valuable. Step 4 is similar to "spring cleaning." We courageously look inside ourselves and find all those "things" that keep us from having a self that feels clean and whole. We also discover forgotten strengths that will help us in our recovery. Rediscovering our strengths is like looking in the pocket of an old pair of jeans and finding a $10 bill!

However, before we can clean and sort through things in our Self we need to list what we have within us. Once we see what is in our individual "closet," our Self, we will better be able to ascertain where we will go with our inventory. As we look at our list of behaviors we will find patterns of behaviors and thought that have been detrimental to us. Other behaviors will need to be mended, altered, or changed.

Our completed inventory will give us a sense of security. We will know exactly where we stand within ourselves and, to some extent, with others. Previously, in the midst of our addictions or compulsions, we hadn't had a true sense of where we stood. We often deluded ourselves into saying and believing that our version of reality was true when it was all part of our denial. Our inventory helps us break through the denial and be honest with ourselves. True, much of what we find will be uncomfortable to face, but it will be in the open and it will be the truth.

In beginning our inventory we need to have humility, which is radically different from humiliation. Humility, speaking the truth about ourselves, is integral to doing good Step work. A good beginning point for speaking truthfully about ourselves begins with accepting our humanity. You may say, "Of course I'm human! What is there to accept about that?" What does being human mean?

Being human means our lives have a beginning and an end. We did not cause ourselves to BE. We have limits to what we can do and what we can control. We have no control over what other people think or feel. We have limited control over how others treat us, our health, our physical selves or events in the world. In other words, we are, by our nature, powerless to cause and affect many things within our lives. However, there is someone who supplies us with power and gives us support and help through the difficult times of our lives. This, of course, is our Higher Power, God. All we have to do to access this power is turn our will and our lives over to God.

Being human also means that we grow and develop

throughout our lives. We make mistakes, but we can learn from our mistakes. We practice what we learn and then we go on to learn more. As we continue to learn we make more errors. Being human means we are in a continual cycle of learning, making mistakes, learning and growing. Unfortunately, our mistakes and those of others can hurt. At times we are so badly wounded we begin to act and to react in unhealthy ways. Being human often means we accumulate wounds and don't know how to allow ourselves to heal.

Step 4 is the beginning of the "How to" on healing our wounds. As we progress through Step 4 we begin to look at ourselves, how we have wounded others, and the ways in which we ourselves have been wounded. We must acknowledge our various wounds so we can begin to grieve our losses—our loss of self, our loss of relationships. Only after we have progressed through the various stages of grief (denial, anger, bargaining, depression and acceptance) can we put these things behind us. Step 4 helps us begin grieving by breaking down our denial about how we have wounded ourselves and others, as well as the ways we have been wounded.

As we list various actions and events we will feel a multitude of feelings. Often the predominant feelings are shame and guilt. All of us have done things that have resulted in feelings of guilt, shame or both. These two feelings, although similar at first glance, are very different and have very different effects upon us.

Guilt is a feeling that occurs when we believe we have done something wrong. The result of "good" guilt is that we will be moved to change our actions. When we say something destructive to someone in an argument we may see the pain in the face of the other person. We may then have wished we hadn't said it. We feel guilty. This guilt can then move us both to apologize and to find other ways to communicate during an argument. "Good" guilt leads to changes in our behavior and the healing of relationships.

"Bad" guilt, an overwhelming sense of guilt that won't leave us no matter what we do, is actually shame. Shame is a feeling that comes from the belief there is something inherently wrong with our very selves. When we feel shame we are working from a belief that we are bad, defective, evil or incapable of good. The belief system that leads to shame is learned at a young age.

Whereas guilt can propel us to do something constructive about our situation, shame often leads to destructive behaviors. If we believe we are not lovable we may set up situations leading to rejection thus proving to ourselves we are unlovable. Shame may prevent us from believing we can get better, that there is hope.

As we work the Steps, we will begin to work through much of our shame and guilt. Each time shame pops up, STOP! Place yourself in your safe place with your Higher Power. Ask your Higher Power to fill you with love and heal the shame. Resolve the guilt by continuing to work the Steps.

There will often be times we write down something and know we were not the only one to blame. There were one or more people who had a role in what happened. It's very tempting to want to place at least some of the blame of what happened on the other person(s). Avoid that temptation. Placing blame is not our job. We are responsible for what we do. Everyone else is responsible for what they do. It is imperative we accept all our responsibility, but only that which is our responsibility. We allow others to accept their responsibility; however, it is not our job to point their faults and failings out to them. We need to work our own program, not someone else's. We take our own inventory and allow others to take their inventory.

At times we will find we have resentments, in which we

relive the original hurt and anger, or grudges against one or more persons because of something they did to us. These resentments can color our lives with negativity and hostility. Resentments have such power that one resentment can permeate everything we do in a large or small way depending upon the strength of the resentment. Recovery demands we let go of resentments.

The first step in releasing ourselves from a resentment is to acknowledge it. Once we look at the resentment and gauge its magnitude, we can decide how to let the resentment go. Some resentments are managed by praying that God give the person who hurt us blessings that we ourselves would like to receive. Most of the time it is very difficult to begin praying for someone who has hurt us. Often we have been so wounded by an individual we first need to pray that God help us become willing to even be willing to pray for the one who has hurt us. As we continue to pray for a particular individual we will find it easier and our resentment will gradually disappear.

Others of us have been so deeply wounded, for example, by abandonment or sexual and physical abuse, that we are not at all able to pray for the one who hurt us. These wounds need to be healed if we are to be whole people. However, we will need the help of a therapist and/or support group as well as our God. God gave us people with skills to help us. Do not be afraid to make use of those who are able and willing to help. Time and patience will be required to cope with the deep pain of various forms of abuse. Rarely does true forgiveness come instantly. Forgiveness is a process. Working the Steps requires only that we be in process.

As we prepare our inventory it is also important to discover those gifts and talents we have but have not been using. When we are in the midst of our addictions or compulsions we do not always see our giftedness. Discovering our strengths can help us find the tools for our recovery. Paradoxically, we often find our giftedness in the same general location as our character defects. For example, one character defect might be that I am stubborn and unyielding. In a negative direction this could lead to my being rigid and inflexible. As I work on this character defect I may discover my gift which is the determination and commitment to do what I believe is right. Another example would be the gift of a loving and giving nature found in the defect of one who is so caught up in doing for others that she or he loses self in his or her actions. Often our character defects are exaggerations in the opposite direction of our gifts, and vice versa.

As you work on your Fourth Step be gentle, yet honest, with yourself. Always remember you are loved and accepted by your Higher Power no matter what is in your inventory.

ESPECIALLY FOR WOMEN

As a woman the chance that you are more acquainted with your weaknesses than your gifts is outstanding. Almost all, if not all, the women I have worked with have little conception of their giftedness, their strengths. Frequently their greatest failings have not been in what they have done to others, but in what they have neglected in themselves.

In our society women are trained to be the caretakers, the nurturers. To be able to nurture others is a tremendous gift; however, to nurture others to the exclusion of self is destructive. We will begin to resent those we nurture. When we do not nurture ourselves we do not become aware of our gifts and talents. We often view ourselves as an object which does for others. We then allow others to treat us as an object. As a result we feel empty and resentful, and may not be aware of why we feel this way.

In working Step 4 spend time on how you have neglected yourself. Identify those gifts you have not given time to develop. Discover your strengths. If you simply can't come up with strengths, ask someone you love and trust. That's risky, but very affirming.

As you are doing Step 4, continually affirm yourself. Remind yourself that God loves you and cares for you just the way you are. Remember that God has given you your gifts and they are yours to use and develop. How have you used them? Do inventory your failings. Don't dwell on them. You have probably dwelled on them most of your life. Do dwell on your giftedness. Most likely very few people have affirmed your gifts.

PRAYER EXPERIENCES

1. Do the relaxation prayer and go into your safe place. Ask your Higher Power to help you with your Fourth Step. Ask your Higher Power to reveal to you things you need to write down. Whatever surfaces within you—write it down. Do not judge it. After you write each thing down, thank your Higher Power for bringing you closer to healing and recovery.

2. Take out your Bible and go to 1 Corinthians 13. Do the relaxation prayer. Slowly read to yourself "the love" chapter substituting your name for the word "love." Does it fit? Jot down the ways your name does not fit. This is a good way to get in touch with character defects. Thank your Higher Power for revealing these things to you and bringing you closer to healing and recovery.

3. During your morning time of prayer and meditation, ask God to point out to you throughout the day your character defects. Jot these down either as they occur, or during your evening time of prayer and meditation.

4. After the relaxation prayer, and when you are in your

safe place ask your Higher Power to point out to you the good things about yourself, your strengths. Write these down.

5. During a period of quiet, go over your list of the qualities you find in your Higher Power. Which of those qualities do you find in some degree, no matter how small, within yourself?

6. Spend time each day doing the relaxation prayer and going to your safe place. Allow your Higher Power to flood you with love and hold you. Allow yourself to feel the love and acceptance your Higher Power has for you just the way you are.

7

STEP 5

Admitted to God, to ourselves and to another human being the exact nature of our wrongs.

Step 5 begins with our fearless and searching moral inventory of Step 4. What do we do with it? As we read it again we notice there are many secrets. Almost every inventory contains at least one item that makes us blush and wish we could deny. Every inventory contains events, personal relationships or characteristics we want to keep secret. Often we have done everything in our power to keep the secrets.

Once we have made our fearless moral inventory, we have to do something with it or the secrets contained in it could overwhelm us with shame. Remember, shame is the feeling that comes from the belief that something is basically damaged or wrong with us. Step 5 provides us the opportunity to cleanse ourselves from our shame by breaking the secrets that bind us and prevent us from being who we are. To break secrets we have to tell secrets.

What kind of secrets do we mean? Very simply we mean anything that would make us cringe and become afraid if someone found out about it. Is there something about yourself you are sure, if people knew, they wouldn't like you? Is there something you have been told not to tell because people just wouldn't understand, or it would bring shame upon the family? Secrets include such things as suicide within the family, alcoholism, prison, mental illness, sexual abuse, drug abuse, physical abuse, adoption, abortion, eating disorders, stealing, rape, lying, cheating—and the list goes on. Secrets are damaging when we keep them buried deep within us. We feel unclean because of those secrets.

When we live in a dysfunctional family, we usually operate by three rules: Don't think. Don't feel. Don't talk. Never were we to think that something was wrong. Never were we to ask why or question what was going on. We were just to accept things the way they were. With the "Don't think" rule came "Don't feel." Frequently we were told our feelings were false, not valid. "You don't feel that way. How could you know how you feel, you're too young!" Often we were told in no uncertain terms we had no right to feel the way we said we felt. The "Don't talk" rule told us to keep the secrets of our family dysfunction. We learned something was wrong with our family and it was a terrible transgression to talk about it.

As we keep the secrets of our family, we isolate ourselves and believe we have the only family with this type of problem. The secrets fester, our shame festers, and we feel as if something is wrong with us. These secrets, which we believe are so terrible, are what bring on the sense of shame, and we will do anything to keep our secrets. They pull us into ourselves and prevent us from revealing ourselves. We isolate ourselves from people. When we don't expose our secrets to the light they take on a dark life of their own and can destroy us. Our secrets can force us to use any means to keep people at a distance. This is why we are only as healthy as our sickest secret. By revealing our secrets to trusted individuals our pain can be validated, and the sense of ourselves as "bad" can be eliminated.

To whom do we tell our secrets? We tell our secrets only

to people we can trust, people who will listen to us, accept us and not judge us. We tell our secrets to people who will hold those secrets gently and tenderly. After all, when we tell our secrets we give away a part of our heart, and we do not want our heart hurt again.

Individuals who have been working the Steps have already been telling secrets. If you are with a competent therapist you are learning the freedom that comes from bringing to light the dark places within you. As you talk and listen in support groups you gain experience in breaking your secrets and helping others to break theirs. These experiences also help you learn how to identify someone who is trustworthy to listen to your Fifth Step.

Step 5 provides a safe place for us to tell our secrets. The first person who hears our Fifth Step is someone with whom we have already begun developing a trusting relationship, our Higher Power. As we have an intimate conversation with our Higher Power about our inventory, we will gain greater understanding, and will begin to see more clearly the patterns of our behaviors. Once we see those patterns we will begin to understand some of the reasons we got into such a mess.

After we admit to God the exact nature of our weaknesses we need to admit them to ourselves. Do not take this part of this Step lightly. It is most difficult to be honest with ourselves. We can delude ourselves better than we can delude anyone else. Ask your Higher Power to help you be honest with yourself as you go over each part of your inventory. When you discover a new pattern or thought or behavior, look at that pattern and admit to yourself it has been a part of your life.

The last part of Step 5 is admitting the exact nature of our faults to one other person. This is scary. All kinds of thoughts go through our heads. "What will she think about me?" "What if I am just as bad as I thought . . . what if I'm worse?!" "No one else is like me." "What will he say?"

This Step is an important part in breaking the shame you carry by breaking the power of your secrets. As you have worked the program and attended meetings you have, hopefully, gained confidence in yourself, as people have given you support and encouragement. You have, by this time, heard many stories similar to yours. You may have wondered how some people knew so much about you without even meeting you. These experiences show you that you are not the only one who has done the things you have done. Chances are your sponsor has done many things you have done, just in his or her own way.

Have courage. Share your secrets. There is healing in the sharing. Of course, it is vital that you choose someone you trust to help you do your Fifth Step. Choose someone with whom you have a good relationship and feel comfortable. Your sponsor would be a good choice. Whoever it is, you should sense she or he has a strong positive regard for you. Know, or have a strong sense, that the person is caring and accepting. You will be very vulnerable during your Fifth Step. Choose someone you can trust with your heart.

Some people come away from their Fifth Step feeling lighter, unburdened. Others, hearing the stories of feeling lighter, are disappointed because they feel worse. You will feel one way or the other, or somewhere in between. If you are one of those who feel worse after your Fifth Step, you may need to talk to someone to discover why this is so. Bring it up in a meeting and listen to what others say. It can be a terrifying experience to reveal to someone, even if we trust that person, a secret of ours. We may still be filled with shame and fear that this person will think differently about us now that we have told our secret. If that is the case go back to that person and talk about the experience. As long as the individual who heard your Fifth Step did not shame you or judge you, you should soon notice a decrease of shame. If you still feel much shame you may have some feelings that need to be resolved with the help of a competent therapist. Sometimes we uncover wounds that still need healing. These will take some time, patience and gentleness on your part.

Occasionally people come back to me because they realized they forgot to mention something in their Fifth Step. Due to anxiety, or the painfulness of the forgotten incident, something was left out. This is a perfectly human experience. There is no need to feel guilt or shame over this situation. Simply rejoice that you are human. Remember, the Steps are not meant to be worked once perfectly. They are to be worked the best that we can each time that we can over the course of our lifetime.

By doing our Fifth Step we again become more open to ourselves, our Higher Power and to other people. Breaking the power of our secrets has the result of cracking the wall around our hearts, allowing love to flow between us and others. Cracking that wall also allows us to continue to heal as we allow ourselves to experience our feelings more deeply.

ESPECIALLY FOR WOMEN

When we admit the nature of our faults contained in our fearless moral inventory, we admit to what we have done and what we have failed to do. Begin by spending time on what you have done, because so often our actions result in the feelings of greatest shame. As we admit to the items on our inventory, they will release their grip on us. That is why we go over our inventory three different times. Each time our shame is loosened.

When we admit to God the exact nature of our errors we discover we have not been struck by lightning. Hopefully we discover we are loved. As we go over our inventory with ourselves we look honestly at the secrets that have held us in bondage for so long. If our Higher Power hasn't struck us down by now, maybe we shouldn't be so hard on ourselves. Remember, part of being human is learning from our mistakes. We can't learn if we don't face up to our mistakes and discover how we could do things differently. Finally, when we tell our inventory to another human being, someone loving and accepting, the power of our secrets to harm us is destroyed, or at least is in the final death throes.

In admitting the nature of our wrongs, we need to spend time admitting to how we have wronged ourselves by not caring for ourselves. Maybe we haven't taken time to discover our giftedness. So often we have used our gifts solely for others, have neglected ourselves, and weren't even aware we were using gifts.

Almost every woman I know has difficulty admitting her giftedness. Women are gifted in so many various areas, but, unfortunately, our society often trivializes the gifts women have developed, such as the ability to nurture. Society often forgets, and even denies, that women have other gifts, such as organizational skills and leadership, which have traditionally been known as male qualities. Although society is coming to realize all human beings, whether they be male or female, have various gifts contained to a greater or lesser degree in each person, women are still not encouraged to develop and claim their own giftedness.

Whatever your giftedness, claim it! Tell God, yourself and one other person about your gifts. Your giftedness is God's gift to you. Your giftedness is part of what makes you a unique human person. When we do not claim our giftedness, we fail to make use of a precious part of ourselves, which results in our not being the individual we were created to be.

Remember that this Step is not to lay blame. This Step is where we admit to the reality of our lives. In the Steps that follow we take positive action to change what we wish to change about ourselves.

PRAYER EXPERIENCES

1. Take your inventory to a place where you can have some quiet. Light a candle or oil lamp and get comfortable. If soft music would help you, put some on. Sit comfortably on the floor or in a chair. Do the relaxation prayer. Invite your Higher Power to sit with you. Go into your safe place if it helps. Go over your inventory with your Higher Power. After you talk to your Higher Power about each item ask your Higher Power for feedback. Listen quietly to what stirs in your heart. Write it down. As you continue, ask your Higher Power to reveal anything you do not already know and need to know. Write it down. Finish by saying whatever else is on your heart and thank your Higher Power for being with you.

2. Again set a meditative atmosphere. You may find it helpful to bring either a mirror or a picture of yourself with you. Do the relaxation prayer. Invite your Higher Power to be with you. Go over your inventory and the various patterns you have discussed. You may want to look at the picture of yourself or look in the mirror as you do this. Say to yourself, "I admit that I have. . . ." Again look for patterns of behavior. When you have finished look at yourself and say, "Yes, I have done these things. These were all part of my past. I will forgive myself. I accept the forgiveness of my Higher Power."

3. After you have done the final part of your Fifth Step go again to where you can be quiet. Bring with you paper, pen, matches and something in which to burn the paper. Do the relaxation prayer and go to your safe place. Ask your Higher Power what part of the Fifth Step your Higher Power would like you to let go of. Write those things down. Place the paper in the receptacle and burn it. Allow your Higher Power to take those things from you. Know that those things are no longer visible either to you or your Higher Power.

8

STEP 6

Were entirely ready to have God remove all these defects of character.

Each previous Step has prepared us to work Step 6. Review the development of your program. First you came to terms with your powerlessness over people, places and things. Next you came to believe a Power greater than yourself could help you, and you made a commitment to your Higher Power. This commitment to One who is love and the source of your own personal power enabled you to look honestly at yourself and tell someone you trusted about those things you discovered about yourself.

With Step 6 we begin to eliminate the character defects which have caused so many problems in our lives. The One who has the power to help us eliminate our character defects is our Higher Power. We have marshalled much courage and strength, and discovered the gift of our personal power, to come this far in the program. We will need God to help us tap into that courage and strength and help us with our character defects.

Step 6 requires a great commitment. We are in this program because the unmanageability of our lives brought us to the point where we had to try something different. Steps 1, 4 and 5 helped us to look at where we have been in our lives. Step 6 asks us to change the direction of our lives by changing our character defects. Steps 2 and 3 provide the strength and the support for us to work this Step.

We will discover that making changes in our old destructive behavior patterns is difficult. We have become accustomed to "our" way of doing things. One very comforting aspect of doing things the "old way" is that we know what will happen when we do things that way. True, we may find ourselves in utter chaos, but at least we are familiar with this chaos. When we try something new, we get a different result. Can we handle the results? There are no guarantees our different method of doing things will have positive results. Our hope, however, is in the fact that if we do something different, something different will occur. For most of us, that something different will be positive.

The Steps do not ask us to be impulsive in trying something different. The program we are working has had positive results since the Big Book (*Alcoholics Anonymous*) was published in 1939. Each of us truly working the Steps has been doing much prayerful introspection. We have begun to look at ourselves in an honest manner. As we examine how we have acted in the past, we can decide how we need to act in the present. The changes we make now are a result of reflection, not impulsivity. Our "doing something different" now has a much greater chance of having a positive result than it did in the past.

Another possible roadblock interfering with the working of this Step is the idea that we must change all our character defects immediately. I'm smiling as I write this because I remember when I felt I had to do just that. However, the feelings I felt at the time did not bring smiles. I knew I would fail; I never would be able to change all my character defects at one time and have those changes last. I felt overwhelmed. Although I feel differently now, I have not changed the way I think. I still believe I will not be able to make all my forever changes right now. The difference, however, is I now know this Step is not asking me to become ready to make all changes immediately and forever.

Part of being human is that we constantly grow and change. As we grow we continually move toward perfection, but we will never attain perfection. All we need to do, and all this Step is asking of us, is to make a commitment to changing and releasing our character defects. As we do this we will become more the person we have the potential to be. We are on a grand adventure to change and discover who we are. We do not do this alone! With this Step we make the decision to enter into partnership with our God and find ourselves. As we progress on our journey we will let go of our character defects as we discover new ways of being and acting.

With Step 6 all we need to do is to become ready to ask our Higher Power to remove our character defects. We don't ask to have them removed at this time. We have to become ready to let them go. The first step in doing anything is having the willingness to do it. Without the desire to change we will not be able to change. Without God we will not be able to change. Our character defects have served a purpose for us, even if they were destructive in many ways. With this Step we develop the willingness to risk losing whatever protection our character defects had for us, and take a chance that we can learn to act in a way that brings us peace and happiness.

How does one develop willingness to change? One way is to form an image of ourselves as we wish to be. If you would like to be known as someone who can express anger appropriately, then begin to form an image of yourself doing exactly that. Take a situation in which you expressed your anger in your old inappropriate manner and imagine the entire situation with you acting the way you would like to act. If you would like to become patient, practice seeing yourself as a patient person. If you want to complete a project imagine yourself doing each step required until you can see in your mind's eye the completed project.

Seeing ourselves as we want to be prevents us from reinforcing our character defects and feeling the old shame again. Seeing ourselves as our "old self" reinforces our old way of acting. Imagining ourselves with our new behaviors reinforces the new us. Seeing ourselves acting the way we want to act helps us believe we can change. As we imagine the changes we become more aware of our personal power given to us by God, who will help us change. The rigidity of our "old" way will dissolve and we become ready to change.

Many times we are reluctant to give up certain character defects because they give us a certain payoff or pleasure. So often our old behaviors are a mixed bag. Drinking and drugging, for example, can temporarily make us feel powerful and in control. Inappropriate use of sex, food and shopping can do the same thing. The "payoff" for these behaviors is the sense of power and control we feel for that very brief period of time. As we work the program we come to realize the payoff has, in reality, been detrimental. We are not more powerful and we do not have greater control. We are, in actuality, less powerful and have less control.

To become ready to have God remove our defects of character we need to realize how the defects have harmed us. The damage caused by our old ways of acting is part of what we learned in our Fourth and Fifth Steps. We want the destruction to stop. Our heart is moved to want to change. We want to build, not destroy. Our desire to change brings us to the willingness of having God remove these defects from us.

ESPECIALLY FOR WOMEN

For many women this Step can be a stumbling block. Letting go of old destructive behavior patterns may mean letting go of certain destructive relationships. What if we actually do change, but the significant other in our life doesn't like the way we've changed? What if our significant other leaves us or becomes so angry with our changes that we are forced to leave? Then where will we be? Alone?

No, not alone. Yes, without that one particular person, but not alone. We will have the people in our support group with whom we have connected. There are now new relationships, new friends, who know us as someone who is gifted and precious. These new friends will remind us how important and valuable we are. They will tell us we deserve warm, positive, loving relationships.

Commitment is important in every relationship. Significant relationships in our lives should only be severed when we have tried all we reasonably could. I do not believe God would ask us to destroy ourselves in the process of continuing a destructive relationship. I cannot believe that God who is love would require us to stay in relationships that would destroy us physically, emotionally and spiritually. This comes from my belief that God is all-loving and wants nothing but the best for all of us.

Another difficulty some women have at this stage in the Steps is believing they could not change even if they wanted to. So many women had it drummed into them from the time of birth that they were incompetent and incapable of doing much of anything. Already you have experienced personal power resulting from your relationship with God who is within you. You have experienced changes. However, old belief systems are difficult to break. If you continue to have this belief system and would like to be rid of it, use affirmations.

First try imagining yourself with your new behavior. If you find that difficult use verbal affirmations. Some good ones would be, "I am a competent and capable person," "I can do anything I put my mind to," and "I have the personal power given to me by God that will effect change in my life." These affirmations help dispel the panic and reinforce the personal power you feel.

Remember, with Step 6 you are not trying to change any defects of character. What you are doing is developing an attitude of willingness. You are not alone. God is with you. Your support group is with you. You can do it!

PRAYER EXPERIENCES

1. Do the relaxation prayer and go into your safe place. As you are there with your Higher Power, hear God say, "You are precious to me. You are gifted. You are able to do anything you want."

2. Do the relaxation prayer and then go into your safe place. Talk with your Higher Power about one of your character defects. Tell your Higher Power how this defect has affected your life. What does holding onto this defect do for you? How does holding onto this defect hurt you? How would your life be different without this character defect?

3. List your character defects on one side of the page. Ask your Higher Power what you can put in the place of this character defect. Opposite the character defect write the new behav-

ior you want to substitute. Imagine a situation in which you are using your new behavior.

4. Spend a few minutes a day quietly asking your Higher Power to help you become ready to have your defects of character removed. Imagine your Higher Power pouring willingness into you. You might want to image the willingness as some color just as you have imaged your Higher Power's love as some color.

9

STEP 7

Humbly asked him/her (God) to remove all our shortcomings.

After we have made ourselves ready to have God remove our character defects, the time has come to ask God to do just that. We do this with humility. We do this, not with resignation or a sense of giving in, but with the freedom that comes from being willing to put ourselves totally at God's will. This is a time of challenge.

The humility with which we ask God to remove our short-comings is an extension of turning our lives and our will over to the care of God (Step 2). Turning our lives and our will over to God required a willingness and a decision to give ourselves to God. We trusted God to care for us, and to do what is best for us. By humbly asking God to remove our shortcomings we are again putting ourselves in God's care. We are again trusting that God will help us, guide us, direct us. We are putting our shortcomings in God's hands and asking God's help in eliminating those shortcomings.

What occurs in our heart and spirit during this Step can cause pain and frustration. The end result, however, is one of new growth. We come to Step 7 similar to a cast-iron skillet encrusted with a heavy black residue. One method of ridding the skillet of this crust is to place the skillet in the flames of a fire. Over a period of hours the crust is burned off and the skillet is like new. In Step 7 we are asking God to burn away the heavy ugly crust caused by our character defects.

The pain and frustration comes when we have difficulty ridding ourselves of our shortcomings. Our human tendency is to want the accomplished fact RIGHT NOW. Frustration occurs when we are working on a particular shortcoming and it keeps popping up no matter what we do. There are times we doubt our progress. Our feelings of failure return.

When these feelings occur—STOP. We need to remember what Step 7 says: "We asked (God) to remove our shortcomings." We work on the Step with God. We cannot do it alone. "Neither could we reduce our self-centeredness much by working or trying on our own power. We had to have God's help."[1] Remember that God will love us no matter how often our shortcomings present themselves. God knows what is in our heart and sees our struggle.

During Step 6 we began to imagine ourselves acting the way we want to act rather than in our old destructive manner. Each time we imagine ourselves acting in a healthy manner we are teaching ourselves how to act. We may not have had good role models when we were children. Now, however, we can parent ourselves through the powerful tool of visual affirmation.

Affirming ourselves with our imagination is much more powerful than verbal affirmations. However, many of us may first need verbal affirmations when we can't seem to imagine ourselves with our new behavior. Our verbal affirmations will begin to change our inner tapes which say we can't be different than we are. Once we are comfortable with verbal affirmations we can proceed to visual affirmations.

When we see things about ourselves we want to change,

our tendency is to try to change everything at once. Remember, character defects were acquired over a lifetime. Even with God's help we cannot rid ourselves of them at once, unless God chooses to work a miracle in us. Without God's help it will be almost impossible to rid ourselves of any of our shortcomings.

As we work with our Higher Power on removing our shortcomings we are continually reminded that our strength, our power, comes from God. If we attempt to rid ourselves of even one defect without our Higher Power, and manage to succeed partially, we begin to believe we did this on our own. A false sense of pride, or grandiosity, develops and we are quickly on our way to relapse. We must always remember the power we have and use to effect change comes directly from our Higher Power who loves us and is within us.

Asking God's help in this matter is not a passive act. We do not just ask, expecting God to do all the work. We also cooperate with the way God works within us helping us eliminate our shortcomings. We must be willing to go into the flames and be cleansed.

As we cooperate with God on removing our shortcomings we will discover other character defects we will need to ask God to remove. The knowledge of these "new" defects will come in a variety of ways. The least painful will be our becoming aware of the shortcoming through our own spiritual journey. We will "hear" God speaking in our hearts bringing us to awareness of another defect.

Another way God speaks to us is through other people. How difficult it is to listen to others tell us about our faults! Not everyone who speaks to us is a messenger from God. However, most of those who know us well, whether they like us or dislike us, do have valid knowledge about us that we can use to grow and develop. Unfortunately, if we are in the throes of our dysfunction we are most likely in relationship with others who are also dysfunctional. The result is that people can tell us our faults in a very hurtful and damaging manner. When we are reeling from a verbally and, therefore, emotionally abusive tirade we are not able to find any immediate truth, if it be present, in what was said. We are in too much pain.

To work through the pain, to heal and to find the truth about ourselves contained in the incident, there are certain steps that can help us. The first is simply to acknowledge to ourselves that we were hurt. So often we try to shield ourselves from the pain we feel by denying the pain is present. We don't want to admit someone can hurt us.

Write about what happened. Include thoughts, feelings, losses and how the event has affected relationships. Take this to God in prayer and pour out your heart. Continue this process until you feel some relief. After some time has passed, days, weeks or longer depending upon how deep the hurt, take the event again in prayer. This time ask God to help you heal and grow from this by helping you find any truth in what was said to you. Take what the person said to you and write it down with different words that have the same message, but stated gently. Look honestly at the new words and decide if there is even a kernel of truth in what is there. If there is truth decide what you can do to change.

Not everything said to us contains truth. There are people who are so wounded themselves that their attacks are pathetic attempts to raise their own sense of self-worth. In such situations the truth to be found is not in what is said to us, but in how we handle the painful situation. Do we respond with equal viciousness or are we able to respond in a manner that protects ourselves but is not retributional? Do we allow ourselves to be continually abused or can we set limits and boundaries to protect ourselves? Do we nurse resentments or are we able to acknowledge our pain, grieve our hurts, and release our resentments? These questions will help us identify other character defects we would like God to remove from us.

Change is a two-part process. When we say we are going to change clothes, everyone assumes we will take off what we are presently wearing and put on something else. In asking God to remove our shortcomings we are asking God to help us change. Just as in changing clothes we will need to put on something new. We cannot rid ourselves of one way of acting without developing another way to act. Part of the process of asking God to remove our shortcomings is also to ask God what to put in their place. As we let go of the old ways of acting, we practice the new.

Again, it is important to remember that getting rid of our character defects and shortcomings is a process that will last our entire lifetime. None of us is perfect. We are very, very human. Accepting our humanity, our fallibility, is one of the important tasks we accomplish as we work these Steps. As we become more at ease with the reality that we are human, we can become more gentle with ourselves as we work in partnership with our Higher Power to effect change in ourselves. We begin to have a greater acceptance of ourselves which will lead to a greater acceptance of others. Serenity will continue to grow in our lives.

As we work with our Higher Power to remove our shortcomings we will find that trust in our Higher Power increases. We are able to believe more deeply that God not only loves us as we are, but also loves us so much that God wants us to heal. God will not love us any less if we do not turn our lives over and do not change. God does, however, call us to growth and serenity. We achieve serenity by putting aside our own self-will and cooperating with God.

The personal power we have discovered by connecting with God aids us in eliminating our shortcomings. As we practice our new behaviors through imaging and interaction with others, we will become more confident and more comfortable with our new selves. Each success increases our trust in God and our confidence in ourselves.

ESPECIALLY FOR WOMEN

Step 7 is an exciting Step. Here we discover another aspect of personal power. We discover we can do marvelous things to change our lives when we work with God, the source of our power. We begin to act with confidence and authority because we now believe we are capable people. We begin using, to an even greater extent, the gifts we uncovered in our Fourth Step.

There is, of course, pain in the process of this change. Many of the people closest to us, family and friends, will think us strange as we change. Some may be threatened by us. We may not be entirely comfortable with our new selves. As we have changed we have lost a relationship with someone close to us, our old self. We need to mourn the loss of our "old" self just as it is important to mourn the loss of any relationship that had been important to us.

One woman, with newly discovered personal power and self-confidence, wrote a letter to her "old" self to tell her good-bye. She was deeply saddened by the loss of her "old" self; after all, she had known her for almost 40 years. In the letter she also thanked her "old" self for protecting her the best way she knew. It was time now to say goodbye, but she truly appreciated that her "old" self had done the best she could. The "new" self forgave her "old" self for the pain resulting from the old behaviors. You, too, may need to write such a letter.

PRAYER EXPERIENCES

1. Bring your journal and Fourth-Step work with you. After the relaxation prayer enter your safe place. Spend time

with your Higher Power sharing whatever is in your heart. When you are ready, ask your Higher Power to reveal to you one or two character defects for you to work on. Write the defects on the top left of a page in your journal. Ask your Higher Power to show you ways in which the character defects are operative in your life. Write these down. On the right half of the page rewrite those examples substituting positive behaviors for your negative behaviors. Ask your Higher Power to point out to you when the character defect is displaying itself and how to begin using your positive behavior.

2. At the end of each day go somewhere quiet. You may find it helpful to do the relaxation prayer. Review your day, looking for ways in which the character defects you are working on displayed themselves. Write down what happened. If you would have liked to have responded differently, write how you would like to have responded. Do not beat yourself over the head. Simply tell your Higher Power you are sorry and ask your Higher Power to continue to be with you. Be sure and write down your successes. Anytime you were able to change your behavior, and acted in a new and different manner, write that down. Give thanks to God for helping you.

3. When struggling with the pain of a wound inflicted by harsh words go into your safe place after the relaxation prayer. Imagine the situation as it was with all the pain and hurt. Ask God to come into the scene and fill it with healing love. See the color of your Higher Power's love cover the entire situation. Ask God to heal the pain and help you learn from what happened.[2]

4. Choose an inner gift of yours that you would like to develop. Imagine incidents in which you are using this particular gift. Thank God for gifting you in such a way.

10

STEP 8

Made a list of all persons we had harmed and became willing to make amends to them all.

As your spiritual awakening increases you will notice an increasing awareness of the people you have hurt through your past negative behavior. The names of various people, as well as the situations which caused the hurt, have probably been popping into your mind as you have worked Steps 4, 5, 6 and 7. With those names come negative feelings, predominately guilt and shame, with some anger and resentment thrown in. For us to continue on our spiritual journey guided by these Steps we need to proceed to the next stage of our spiritual "cleansing." Step 8 gives us the two-part plan needed to proceed.

The first part of this process is to make a list of those we have harmed through our addictions or compulsions. In a way, this sounds fairly easy. Most of us are well aware of those we have hurt; often they have loudly made themselves known. We will be able to list these names with little thought, although with some pain.

There are other people that may also need to be included on this list. These are the names of those involved in situations in which we also have been hurt. We might rationalize not placing some names on our list by saying, "It wouldn't have happened if she hadn't . . ." or "I would have never done that if only he had. . . ." Blaming only impedes our recovery. My Grandpa Chapman used to say, "You are never a failure until you blame others for your mistakes." We can only learn from our mistakes if we accept them as ours and discover how we can, in the future, act in a different manner.

An additional method of surfacing names for our Step 8 list is to call to mind all the people with whom we are angry or toward whom we hold resentments. Examine your feelings toward others beginning with family members, significant others and present friends, and then other people from your past. If discomfort, anger or resentment wells up in your chest and throat, add that person to your list. "Why?" you may ask, especially if that person has harmed you and you don't believe you had anything to do with what happened.

In reality we are rarely free from any blame or responsibility in most situations. Almost always we have played a role that has made the situation worse by our behavior. Events to be automatically excluded from personal responsibility are those in which we were physically, sexually and emotionally abused as children. There are, of course, those times as adults, when things happened to us just because we were the one there, e.g., sexual assault, sexual harassment, muggings, robbery, etc. However, for the most part, we share responsibility in whatever action or event we still feel resentment about.

There will be other names you need to add to your list but have blocked or forgotten for one reason or another. These names will eventually come to mind as you continue working the Steps. This is not your one and only time to work on Step 8. Do the best you can at this time but don't worry if you don't do it perfectly. Imperfection only means you are human!

After the list is developed we can progress to the second part of Step 8. We now work on becoming willing to make amends. Often we are already willing to make amends to many people on our list. We are deeply grieved that we have caused so much pain and suffering to those we love. But, for others on our list, becoming willing to make amends is very difficult because of the anger and resentments we hold toward those people. Frequently, the negative feelings we have toward others protect us from something. Very possibly those feelings protect us from being hurt again. However, the negative feelings can generalize to large groups of people and act as a barrier between us and others. We will have a difficult time developing intimate relationships. What a tragedy not to allow ourselves to experience love and, yes, the pain that comes from loving.

Anger and resentment also protect us from the need to humble ourselves and be the one to reach out first, which often goes against our nature. Our pride frequently tells us not to forgive until the other person approaches us. However, this type of pride keeps our resentments boiling and is a barrier to our recovery. We cannot become truly healthy and spiritually alive when we harbor resentments. Resentments have a way of poisoning our very selves. We can become impatient, short-tempered and abusive toward everyone, including ourselves. Resentments also allow an event in the past to continue to have power over us in the present. How can we possibly fully enjoy the present if it is so affected by the negatives in our past? We free ourselves from the past by releasing it and forgiving those who have hurt us.

The entire process of forgiveness is painful and, ultimately, freeing. The stages of forgiveness[1] are similar to those of grieving. We first have to admit we have been hurt. I have a difficult time with this initial stage. I don't like admitting there are people in my life who have the power to hurt me. My choice to love and be loved has given people that power. For me, it is easier to admit I am angry. When I get in touch with my anger, I then look more deeply within myself and find that I am hurting.

After I admit I'm hurt I allow myself to feel the pain. I can then begin to heal.

The next stage is to get in touch with my anger on a deeper level. Being angry is a healthy and normal response to emotional pain, just as physical pain is a healthy and normal response to a broken leg. In the stage of anger it is important to recognize the reasons why we are angry. Usually there are many additional feelings that come with our being hurt, e.g., embarrassment and shame, and we don't like to experience these uncomfortable feelings. We need to admit to ourselves the various elements that add to our emotional pain and allow ourselves to be angry. We need to talk with someone or journal about our anger.

As we move through our anger we begin to think about what we could have done or said differently. We may make excuses for ourselves or the other person. This is the bargaining stage. After we move through this stage we often become depressed, and there is much self-blame in this stage. We become angry with ourselves and may emotionally beat up ourselves. Although it is important to acknowledge the feelings and losses we have experienced due to the hurt, we need to hold those hurts gently so we can let them go. Finally, we come to the point where we can accept the pain, accept the individual who hurt us and proceed with our lives. At this stage of acceptance we can forgive on a deep level.

As you can see, forgiveness is not a quick simple process. We will go through these stages more quickly for a small hurt than we will for a deep wound. Let us give ourselves time. We are on the road to recovery as long as we are allowing ourselves to feel and move through the various stages of grieving.

Becoming willing to make amends involves the process of forgiveness. Early in the healing process we may need to pray, "Make me willing to become willing to forgive." By becoming willing to make amends we are practicing humility. Remember, humility is speaking the truth about oneself. When we become willing to make amends we are stating that we, who are fallible human beings, are willing to admit our fallibility and to accept another's fallibility. Through this program we come to look honestly at our faults and failings. We work to right those characteristics within ourselves that have caused those faults and failings.

Step 8, as does every Step, demands rigorous honesty. Part of that honesty is admitting that we need to forgive ourselves just as much as we need to forgive others. Each of us has done things we wish we could change and for which we are ashamed. God forgives us no matter what we have done. We also need to forgive ourselves. As we are able to accept ourselves and one another as we are, we will discover we have achieved greater serenity. Our spiritual awakening continues.

ESPECIALLY FOR WOMEN

Women, for the most part, have little trouble in listing the people they have hurt. We have been trained to be caretakers. When a relationship fails we have a tendency to believe the failure was solely our fault. Many of us are carrying a burden of heavy responsibility for failed relationships. Much of the burden is warranted, but much is not. We need to forgive ourselves for that which is our responsibility and forgive others for that which is theirs.

In all the time spent on relationship there is one relationship that we women frequently neglect—the relationship with ourselves. Although we have been trained to be caretakers of others, we have neglected the care of ourselves. Now is the time for all women to place our own names on the list of people we have harmed. Now is the time to become ready to make amends to ourselves. For some of us this will feel strange and uncomfortable. We are, however, valuable and precious human beings who deserve some tender loving care. If we can't give ourselves the TLC we need, how can we expect others to do so?

PRAYER EXPERIENCES

1. Do the relaxation prayer and go into your safe place. Ask your Higher Power to point out to you people to whom you need to make amends. Write down those names. Next to each name write down why you need to make amends.

2. Choose someone on your list to whom you are not yet willing to make amends. Either take a picture of the person or write the individual's name down on a piece of paper. Place this picture or paper in a place where you can see it. During your daily prayer and anytime you see the person—the name or the picture—ask your Higher Power to help you to become willing to make amends to this person. Pray daily that this individual receives the spiritual gift that you most want to receive. Continue until your heart has changed and you are now ready to make amends. Repeat the process for each person on your list.

3. Pray daily for each person on your list, asking your Higher Power to fill each individual with healing love.

4. Do the relaxation prayer and imagine yourself with God and the person toward whom you hold resentments. Ask God to fill that individual with love. See the color of God's love totally surround and fill that person.

5. Do the relaxation prayer and imagine yourself with God and a person who has caused you some type of harm. Imagine any resentments as an ugly fence, such as rusty barbed wire, between the two of you. Ask God to break that ugly bond

and cover both of you in love. See the love surround and fill the two of you.

6. If you are having difficulty believing you are important enough to make amends to yourself, go to your safe place. Spend some time with God. See God touch you and fill you with love. Hear God call you by name and say, "I love you. You are more precious to me than you will ever know."

11

STEP 9

Made direct amends to such people wherever possible, except when to do so would injure them or others.

Many of us find it very difficult to tell someone, "I'm sorry." It's much easier to admit to ourselves, to God and to one other person (Step 5) that we had done something, rather than to apologize to the one we had hurt. How humbling it is to admit to the one hurt that we were wrong. How freeing it is! No longer do we feel uncomfortable at the thought of the individual, or turn in another direction when we see the person coming. Often relationships can be healed and friendships begun again. At other times we feel lighter because a burden has been lifted. Frequently, the gnawing pain inside us decreases or is eliminated, removing one of our rationalizations for engaging in addictive behavior.

Making direct amends is an event we prepare for with thought and prayer. Impulsively making direct amends could do tremendous damage. There are times when opening an old wound may cause more harm than good. There are other times when making direct amends could hurt someone else much more than keeping it to ourselves (as in apologizing to your friend for having an affair with his or her spouse when your friend knew nothing of the affair). At other times making direct amends could put us in danger. Apologizing to someone who is not in recovery, and has a history of being physically or emotionally abusive, could lead to being deeply hurt in some way.

If there is any question at all about whether a direct amend should be made find some trusted individual, i.e., sponsor, therapist, who can help you think through the situation. Do this even if you have a question on what appears to be a fairly trivial situation. We do not always know the magnitude of pain associated with another person's hurt. We need an objective person to give us guidance. There are times when it is better to leave old wounds unopened. Of course, there are times old wounds can be healed by our reaching out to make direct amends even when this is uncomfortable or moderately painful to us.

This particular Step carries much personal responsibility. Although we may seek and receive advice from another about whether to make an amend, we are the sole judge of whether we should do this. If we decide not to make a direct amend we must have a clear and definite reason why we have arrived at that decision. Because it is such a humbling experience to make amends, being the human beings we are, we may try to rationalize away having to approach an individual. Our tendency to avoid the painful is the best reason to speak with a trusted individual about our thoughts. We do not want to run the risk of fooling ourselves as we have done so often before. Again, rigorous honesty is mandatory.

How do we make direct amends? Often we can do this by a simple, honest and forthright apology. It is amazing what a simple apology can do to clear the air. Other amends may be more involved. If we have spread an untruth about someone we will need to go to those we spoke to and state the truth. If we have stolen we will need to return what we have stolen, or the value of what we have stolen. Whatever we do to make direct amends, we must do one other thing. We must change our behavior. It is of little profit to us if we apologize for some offense and continue the offending behavior. (If we find we continue to repeat our hurtful behavior we have confronted a character defect we need to ask our Higher Power to remove— Step 7.)

There are times when the person we apologize to does not accept our apology and her or his anger does not diminish. This is very painful for all involved. We must realize, however, that we do not make amends to manipulate the other person into forgiving us and not being angry with us. We make amends because we must do so for our own recovery and our own spiritual development. We have no control over another person's feelings. Of course, our desire is to be at peace with those who impact our lives, but we cannot force any person to accept that peace. All we can do is offer our apology and make whatever amend is necessary. Let us not become angry with someone because they are not able to accept our apology. It will be of no benefit to us to become resentful at another's inability to forgive. We need only concern ourselves with our willingness to forgive. As much as we may disagree with how another individual reacts, each of us must handle our own pain in our own way.

Although Step 9 calls for direct amends, often we feel a need to make an amend when there is no way to do so. The individual may have moved away or died, or it would have caused more harm if we made a direct amend. In many cases the most we can do is admit to God, ourselves and one other person what had happened and change the behavior that caused the problem. In other situations we may be able to make amends indirectly by helping someone who is in a similar situation to the person we had harmed. Whatever method we choose, we must put our whole selves into making the amend.

Frequently amends help us forgive ourselves for our harmful actions. Making amends brings closure to the situation. However, there are times when the natural consequences of our actions are to live with the regret that we have harmed someone. Nothing we do can bring back a life, make someone walk again, or bring healing to an individual who was deeply wounded by our actions. In these situations we need to ask forgiveness from God and others, accept forgiveness, forgive ourselves, change our behavior and continue with our lives.

Often we need to make amends to ourselves. Our behavior has hurt others and has hurt ourselves. We know we have hurt ourselves because we have felt alienated from ourselves. We have already begun amends to ourselves by connecting with our Higher Power, eliminating the addictive substance or compulsive behavior from our lives, working on our relationships and taking care of ourselves. As we continue the Steps we will continue making amends to ourselves by being honest and forthright, establishing healthy and well-balanced relationships and deepening our spirituality. The energy that results from making amends to others and ourselves propels us forward to continue our growth.

ESPECIALLY FOR WOMEN

Making amends to ourselves involves changing our behavior. How often have you had plans to do something for yourself and changed them because someone else wanted to do something different? Now is the time to begin putting yourself at the top of your list. Feel selfish?

If we always place ourselves last we have no time to grow emotionally or spiritually. As you know, from working this program, personal growth takes time. We have had to set aside time to attend meetings and to pray and meditate. Time was needed to establish our relationship with God. If we don't take time for ourselves we grow bitter and resentful. These feelings then spill over to others. Our relationships begin to sour. Our life feels in chaos. We lose our grounding in God and our sense of personal power.

We now have personal experience of the results of placing ourselves first on our priority list. Not only are we happier but our relationships are healthier. We can handle the stresses of daily life with greater ease. We don't take things out on those around us when something goes wrong. When necessity dictates placing ourselves last for a time, we don't resent it. Almost everyone seems happier.

In addition to taking time for ourselves we need to forgive ourselves. We may not have been the wife, mother, daughter or friend someone needed. We cannot change the past. We can accept the past and learn from our mistakes. In the present we do the best we can to live the lessons we have learned. In this way we make amends to ourselves.

PRAYER EXPERIENCES

1. Bring to your prayer the list of persons from Step 8. Do the relaxation prayer and go into your safe place. Ask your Higher Power to reveal to you the ways in which you need to make amends to each person on your list. Discuss with your Higher Power how you would like to make amends. Listen quietly for your Higher Power's response.

2. Do the relaxation prayer and go into your safe place. Ask your Higher Power to fill the person you had harmed with healing love. Ask your Higher Power to heal that individual of the pain and harm brought on by the situation you have in mind. You may find yourself drawn to pray often for the same individual. Listen to the quiet inner voice that calls you to pray in this manner.

3. Do the relaxation prayer and go into your safe place. Write a letter to someone who, for whatever reason, you cannot make direct amends. Say whatever you would like to say to that person. Read the letter to your Higher Power. Imagine reading the letter to the other person. Pray for the individual.

4. Do the relaxation prayer and go into your safe place. Form two images of yourself—one is your new healthier Self and the other is your old unhealthy Self. Have your old unhealthy Self ask forgiveness of your healthier Self for the things you have done to hurt others and yourself. Listen to your healthier Self respond and give forgiveness to your old Self.

12

STEP 10

Continued to take personal inventory and when we were wrong promptly admitted it.

What we have done, to this point, is lay the groundwork for our spiritual development. We have acquired tools to help keep us sober and balanced. Now all we have to do is continue to use these Steps in our day to day lives. Our spiritual awakening has, by this time, become apparent to us and to others. We have begun to "feel" different. We have become more confident and aware of our personal power as we have accepted our powerlessness over people, places and things and turned our lives over to God. As we have felt loved and accepted by God we have come to like ourselves more. Other people respond to us in a different, more positively genuine manner. Our relationships have become healthier. To continue our growth we need to continue the positive habits that will allow us to practice these Steps daily.

Step 10 is the first of the three maintenance Steps. These are what we use on a daily basis to continue our life on the course we have now set. Often, when we get to this point in the 12-Steps, we breathe a sigh of relief. We believe we are almost finished. Some of us even make the mistake of thinking, "Now

I can concentrate on other things in my life." The truth is that when we get to this point in the Steps we have just begun. We have learned most of the principles this program requires. Now we need to practice these principles daily. As we form the positive habit of working these Steps we will not consciously need to focus on what we do, since the Steps will become second nature. Just as our negative behaviors and thoughts appeared to be "part of us," our new behaviors and thoughts can now be "part of us." We will be attuned to a new positive energy within our lives which has resulted from our spiritual awakening. When we notice that this new energy or serenity is lacking, we will know we need to focus on the Steps and return to this simple but powerful plan for our lives.

Step 10 reinforces how important it is to take daily inventory of our lives. Practicing rigorous honesty has been difficult. There was a certain bliss in not looking deeply and honestly at ourselves. If denial did not have its rewards we would not have used it for so long. None of us enjoys seeing our weaknesses. Many of us also have a difficult time discovering our strengths! In Step 10, as we daily practice the Fourth and Fifth Steps, we continue to come in contact with what we have done and what we have failed to do. Our regular daily inventory helps keep us from becoming complacent. Our old character defects can sneak up on us when we aren't paying attention and we get cocky. Beware of times of stress! These are the times we are most prone to slip back into our old destructive behavior patterns.

What can be even more exasperating, as we try to correct a particular character defect, is to overcorrect and develop a character defect to what we were trying to correct! We are learning through this program how to balance our lives. If our character defect is impatience we do not want to become so "patient" we allow people to walk all over us. On the other hand, if our character defect is always trying to please others, losing ourselves in the process, we don't want to overreact and become oppositional. Extremes are generally character defects we need to correct, and which cause relationship problems with others or ourselves. By daily examining our lives through Step 10 we can catch the extremes in our lives and correct them.

Step 10 also reminds us to admit our offenses toward others and promptly make amends. As difficult as this can be it is much easier in the long run. We have already done our major spiritual and emotional housecleaning. When we immediately make amends we don't have our offense weighing heavily on our conscience. By immediately saying, "I'm sorry," we don't have a wounded relationship festering into an infected sore that is difficult to heal. By immediately admitting to our Higher Power we have made a mistake, and then accepting forgiveness, we remain open to the work of God within us. Being honest with ourselves and others gives us a greater sense of self-respect, an attribute that had been sadly lacking in most of us.

As we review our day we also need to examine those times when we neglected opportunities to use our gifts and talents. Notice, also, when gifts and talents *were* used. As we become more aware of our giftedness we will use our gifts rather than our character defects. When we finish our daily inventory we ask forgiveness and give thanks for the day.

As we continue to work the Steps we continue to grow. Our awareness of ourselves, others and our Higher Power increases. We become more peaceful and more aware of our God-given personal power. We are able to allow ourselves to be human with our faults and foibles, and accept the humanity of others. As we continue to grow in awareness of ourselves we will, from time to time, discover patterns of thought and behavior that are not what we want for our "new" selves. These patterns have probably always been present but we did not have the necessary awareness to realize the exact nature of what we were doing. Our Higher Power has blessed us with this new awareness so that we can continue our growth. Our daily inventory will aid us in increasing our awareness of ourselves.

Step 10 reminds us that living the Steps is a daily part of our lives. In fact, it becomes so daily we do not consciously notice when we are doing it. Our new behavior patterns have become part of us. Just as we eat when we are hungry, we touch base with God throughout the day. Immediately attempting to rectify a relationship problem becomes second nature to us. Not that it becomes so easy to say, "I'm sorry," that we become flippant about the event, but we learn the necessity of keeping our lives healthy and balanced. We have now cultivated positive habits to replace destructive habits.

ESPECIALLY FOR WOMEN

The personal power discovered through this program will increase as we continue the behavior patterns we are now learning. Our relationships will continue to grow and develop. Our sense of Self as woman, strong as well as gentle, independent as well as relational, increases. We derive great satisfaction from the gifts God has given us.

Since we have done the major work of admitting past wrongs and making amends for those wrongs, we can now spend time and energy on the present. We will find it easier to apologize when we are wrong. We will also avoid taking on blame when things are not our fault. Our time and energy can be spent enjoying life.

PRAYER EXPERIENCES

1. After each day do the relaxation prayer and go into your safe place. Ask your Higher Power to help you review the day. There in your safe place ask the following questions: What

were the high points of my day? What were the low points of my day? What did I do today to hurt myself, someone else, or my relationship with God? What opportunities did I have today to help someone but didn't? When did I help someone? Write down your responses.

2. When you are reviewing your day look specifically at character defects you are trying to alter. Where did those character defects present themselves today? Where did you find yourself using healthy alternative behavior?

3. Do the relaxation prayer and go into your safe place. Thank your Higher Power for giving you the necessary gifts (courage, strength, persistence) to live your life in a positive manner.

13

STEP 11

Sought through prayer and meditation to improve our conscious contact with God as we understood him (her), praying only for knowledge of his (her) will for us and the power to carry that out.

In Step 11 we continue Steps 2 and 3, but with more structure and on a deeper level. As with many of the other Steps, this Step has several parts to it. We begin with prayer and meditation. What exactly is prayer and meditation? Prayer can be defined as a conscious connecting with God through thoughts and words, or a focusing of our attention on our Higher Power. When I was growing up I was taught that prayer was the lifting of our minds and hearts to God. Words are not necessary in prayer. Our being conscious of the presence of God is all that is necessary. God is well aware of what is in our hearts.

One way to pray is to do and say things for God. For instance, something as simple as working in the yard, driving to work, or going shopping can be prayer if we do this for God. When we turn our lives and wills over to God we turn everything over, including shopping, working, caring for children and making love. Therefore, everything can be prayerful if we consciously place it in God's hands. Our goal in our spiritual life is to be continually aware of God's presence. Of course, this goal is only reached in perfection, and that we will never attain. As has been said in many a meeting, "We strive for progress, not perfection."

It is best to have a regular schedule for prayer and meditation. As we grow and develop spiritually we can modify our spiritual program to suit our changing needs. When first initiating a spiritual program begin the day with prayer and meditation. Simply sit quietly with a meditation book, the Bible, or another spiritual reading book. Begin by asking God to be with you during this time of quiet. Slowly and quietly read to yourself the selection you have chosen. Spend a few minutes reflecting on what is contained in your reading. What meaning does it have for your life? In your journal write what you have learned from your meditation. Ask God to be with you today. If there is anything in particular you would like to work on, ask God to help you. Affirm that you are powerless over people, places and things (Step 1) and that there is One who is both powerful and the source of all power (Step 2) to whom you give your life (Step 3). You may want to end with the Serenity Prayer. Later, perhaps in the middle of the day, just recall that God is with you. Give thanks for what has happened in your day to this point. Ask for any assistance you feel you need. At the end of the day review what has happened using one of the ways suggested in the prayer experiences of Step 10. Again give thanks for your day and ask for forgiveness where necessary.

As we work this Step we will come to a greater conscious contact with God as we understand God. Put simply, we will become more attuned to God's presence in our lives and in our world. God, as we understand God, will become a constant companion. We will begin to see how God works in our lives in so many various ways. We will become more conscious of the beauty in the world. Various events throughout our day will remind us we have put ourselves in God's hands. Greater peace and serenity will come to us. More frequently we will be able to release the control over people we have always tried to have and allow God to take over.

As we become more open to God our serenity increases as we grow and develop spiritually. We find ourselves becoming more tender-hearted which leads to a greater awareness of the pain and evils in the world. Often we will want to do something about what we see. Many times the most we can do is speak out against it. We are powerless over so much of what is going on in the world. There will be times when we will feel drawn to take action on some of the problems we see around us. Simply ask God what is God's will for you, and for the power to carry it out.

Our conscious contact with God usually develops over a period of time. Just as we learn and grow in our ability to practice these Steps, so also do we grow in our relationship with God. So often people are discouraged because they immediately want the peace and serenity they see in others. Hopefully, you have begun to experience peace and serenity. If not, keep working the Steps. Remember that most of us do not have a sudden spiritual experience. Most of us have a quiet realization of our spiritual development. Just as working the Steps is a process, so also is our spiritual development. We need to be patient.

When we work Step 11 we will find the manner in which we pray is different. Most of us used to pray by asking God to do certain things for us, to change us or, more often, to change someone else. The purpose of the prayer in Step 11 is very different. Praying according to Step 11 is another way of abandoning ourselves into the hands of God. We pray only for the knowledge of God's will for us. We wait to hear what that will is. We do not tell God what we believe that will for us should be. Instead of trying to direct our lives we ask God to do that. We simply wait until God delivers the message. Once we have a sense of God's will for us we then pray for the power to carry it out.

For many people their spiritual journey leads them to make a decision to find a church. Some have returned to the church of their childhood. Others found a different church, and still others found a church for the very first time. There appears to be a yearning within most of us human beings that draws us to worship with other people. This is a yearning for community. If you are feeling that yearning ask God to direct you. If you feel anger when you think of "church," examine resentments toward church or religion. Resentments in this area are just as destructive as resentments in other areas of our lives. Pray for God's will for you in this area of your life.

Our spiritual journey affects every area of our lives. Human beings are not people who can put each area of their lives in little compartments that will not affect other areas. In fact, it was our efforts to do exactly that which brought us so much pain. Our spirituality will determine how we treat ourselves and others, as well as how open we are to doing what is necessary to heal. Growing is difficult and painful. By building our spiritual selves we will find that we have also, with the help of God, reconstructed our emotional selves. I firmly believe that God's will for each of us is emotional and spiritual health. By following our spiritual program we will be continually on the road to health.

ESPECIALLY FOR WOMEN

Not only do men and women relate to each other differently, but they also relate to God differently. That is why it is important for you as a woman to discover who God is for you and not as defined by a man. This is not to say that a man's concept of God is not right. It just may not be right for you.

Let your guides in this area be other women. There are books written by women which discuss the feminine nature of God and women's spirituality. Read them. Try some of their suggestions. See how their concepts of God fit into your own spirituality. Gather together a group of women and share your spiritual journey with each other. Such a group can be life-giving. Listen to God who is within you speak to your heart. Trust that message and follow it.

PRAYER EXPERIENCES

1. When sitting quietly during your daily meditation write down the thoughts, feelings, or images that come to you. What do these images mean to you? What direction do you think God is asking you to go?

2. When trying to make a decision about God's will for your life begin with the relaxation prayer and go into your safe place. Talk with God about the decision you are struggling with. If you need to make a choice between two or more options talk about each option with God. Listen to how you feel in your gut about each option. Write about how you feel—your fears, your hopes and dreams. You may need to do this several different times. Ask God for help and then trust that you will make the best decision possible.

3. When praying for the power to carry out a decision go into your safe place. Ask your Higher Power to give you the power to carry out your Higher Power's will. See yourself receiving the power from your Higher Power. Visualize the power in some color coming into you. See yourself doing what you believe you are called to do in partnership with your Higher Power.

14

STEP 12

Having had a spiritual awakening as the result of these Steps, we tried to carry this message to others, and to practice these principles in all our affairs.

Ah, Step 12. Is this the end? As you have probably discovered by now, Step 12 is not the end, only the beginning. Step 12 is a summation of the previous eleven Steps in one simple sentence. All but the middle phrase of this Step, "we tried to carry this message to others" is contained in the previous Steps.

Yes, a spiritual awakening has occurred. Our lives are very different from what they were when we first began this program. What is remarkable is that the events surrounding our lives may be just the same. There may be the same turmoil swirling around us. The difference is within ourselves. We look at life differently. We have learned we are powerless over chemicals and other people. We cannot control most of the events in our lives. We have learned we can have serenity and peace by turning everything over to God as we understand God.

Caring about people is still very important to us. We have learned that our caring and compassion, although it cannot force people to change, can give people the emotional space and acceptance they need to change. As we have learned to accept ourselves we have learned to accept others. The only person we can change is ourself, and even some areas of ourself we cannot change but only accept.

As we have learned to put every facet of our lives in the care of God, we have discovered freedom from the inner turmoil that previously made our lives a living hell. Yes, we still have problems. However, the way we view those problems and the way we handle those problems have changed. We realize we can't control many things outside ourselves, but we are more aware of and make use of our personal power. Through this power we are able to work with God to effect change in our lives. The center of our lives has become our Higher Power, God, and we place our trust in God. Serenity is the result.

When we began to see the difference this spiritual program made in our lives we wanted to tell other people about it. In meetings we talked about what had happened to us. We shared with those who were struggling to come to grips with their own addiction, or the addiction of a loved one, what we had learned as we worked this program. We explained that this program will only change the one working it. This program is not worked as a manipulative tool to change someone else. The only piece of advice we are able to give that we know works is, "Begin working the Steps. Go to meetings." Through all our pain and our sorrow we have learned that working the Steps has been the key to our own peace of mind.

As we tell others about this program we share our own struggles and the methods we used to cope with those struggles. We also shared our own struggles with the program and how difficult it was to do Step 1 . . . then Step 2 . . . then Step 3 . . . then. . . . Each Step had its own special difficulties for each of us. There were times we thought we had one particular Step well in hand only to discover, in working that Step, that we took the principles of that Step to a deeper level.

Throughout we struggled with control. Continually we were turning things over to God. How easy it was to take things back from God without even being aware we had done so! These and other struggles we share with people; not in the sense of giving advice, but in the sense of giving them a story they could relate to. We have no advice to give except to work these Steps the way each person needs to. Hopefully sharing our story will help others see that they, too, can work these Steps. We, also, were at the beginning. We, also, were in great pain. We, also, thought that if we tried just one more thing then the pain would go away. For us, that one more thing was the 12-Steps. This is the message we carry.

We carry this message not only through our words, but also through our deeds. People can see the difference in us. "Walk the talk." We "practice these principles in all our affairs." These principles are the preceding eleven Steps. We continue to work the Steps every day of our lives. Every morning we go over Steps 1, 2 and 3. We continue to imprint the Steps and the principles involved firmly on our minds and hearts. Each morning we go to God and acknowledge God as the source of our personal power. We ask God to remove our character defects (Step 6).

This will be a lifelong process guided by the loving and gentle hand of our Higher Power. At the end of the day we take our inventory and make amends when necessary (Step 10). Throughout the day we communicate with our Higher Power (Step 11). By doing each of these things every day we will continue to grow and develop. Where we had previously had crisis and inner turmoil as a constant companion, we now are grounded in God's love and experience serenity.

Yes, we still experience pain. People can still hurt us and we can still hurt others. Tragedies will continue to come our way from time to time. That is the nature of life. Now, however, we know where our power resides. With our Higher Power as our constant companion we have courage in the face of tragedy, and serenity when confronted with trials.

What a difference 12-Steps make!

ESPECIALLY FOR WOMEN

By now we have come to a stronger more positive image of ourselves as women and as human beings. We have discovered or rediscovered many of our gifts. We have a firmer sense of ourselves as both nurturer and leader, life-giver and limit setter, person of independence and person of interdependence. Our gentleness and compassion spring from our deep inner strength. This we now know.

In discovering ourselves we found we did have qualities traditionally attributed to women: nurturer, care-giver, compassionate and gentle among others. However, we also discovered we had qualities traditionally attributed to men: leadership, stamina, strength, intelligence and many more.

As we continue to work the Steps we will continue to discover, own and develop our giftedness. There will be times, many times, when we will need to acknowledge our shortcomings and make amends. Ironically, our shortcomings will often be in the area of not acknowledging and using our giftedness.

By continuing to work the Steps we will continue the quest of self-discovery and healing. We will also lead others, by the testimony of our lives, to the journey of healing and self-awareness.

PRAYER EXPERIENCES

As you continue to grow spiritually you may want to try new and different ways to pray.

1. Ask your Higher Power to be with you in a special way. Do the relaxation prayer. Very quietly say either the name you call your Higher Power, i.e., God, Jesus, Father, Mother, etc., or a quality of your Higher Power, such as love or peace. Let this word fill your whole being. Whatever thoughts come to your mind gently let them go and return to your special word.

2. Spend some quiet time in nature enjoying the peace that surrounds you. Give thanks to your Higher Power for giving you all that you now see.

3. Keep with you a meditation book of some sort. When you find yourself caught waiting unexpectedly, pull out your book and do some reading.

4. When you find yourself waiting, use the time to ask God to fill the people around you with love . . . even the obnoxious ones. Just see God's love surround them and fill them.

5. Every chance you get say, "Thank you," to God.

NOTES

Chapter 2

1. "Bill's Story," in *Alcoholics Anonymous*, 1976, Alcoholics Anonymous World Services, Inc., p. 8.
2. "There is a Solution," in *Alcoholics Anonymous*, 1976, Alcoholics Anonymous World Services, Inc., p. 25.
3. "How it Works," in *Alcoholics Anonymous*, 1976, Alcoholics Anonymous World Services, Inc., p. 60.

Chapter 9

1. "How It Works," in *Alcoholics Anonymous*, 1976, Alcoholics Anonymous World Services, Inc., p. 62.
2. My thanks to Matthew and Dennis Linn for this prayer. *Healing Life's Hurts: Healing Memories through Five Stages of Forgiveness*, 1978, Paulist Press.

Chapter 10

1. For a complete guide of healing through forgiveness, see *Healing Life's Hurts: Healing Memories through Five Stages of Forgiveness*, 1978, Paulist Press, by Matthew Linn and Dennis Linn. This discussion on the stages of forgiveness is based upon the material in their book.